stories for your Soul

ORDINARY PEOPLE. EXTRAORDINARY GOD.

ALSO BY MAX LUCADO

stories for your Soul

ORDINARY PEOPLE. EXTRAORDINARY GOD.

MAX LUCADO

THOMAS NELSON
Since 1798

CONTENTS

CONTENTS

INTRODUCTION

I have a verse written on the interior of my Bible. **"He always used stories to teach them" (Mark 4:34** ICB**).** Jesus didn't *occasionally* use a story. He didn't *every so often* use a story. He *always* used stories. You could count on Christ to have a good story in his hip pocket. Sometimes he added an application. Sometimes he just related the story. But he always had a story.

Don't you like stories? Doesn't the phrase "Once upon a time . . ." pique your interest? As a preacher, I've learned the power of an illustration. When the audience grows heavy eyed and droopy jawed, I just need to say, "Let me tell you a story," and the dead are raised. People perk up. We love a story.

I suppose that's why I have so many of them. What art collectors do with paintings, I do with stories. I keep them framed and hung in the gallery of my memory.

May I take you on a tour?

Let me tell you some stories.

A story about a homeless man and the sister who sought him out.

A story about the happiest man in Bermuda.

A story about the MS victim whose list of blessings was three times longer than his list of concerns.

A story about the blind football player who snapped the ball.

I've included a few of my favorite personal stories too.

Story after story.

I hope you enjoy them. Even more, I pray that these stories spark an appreciation for the greatest story of all, the story of Jesus. God on earth. God in the flesh. God in a manger, in a workshop, in the midst of this turbulent world. No story compares to his. Jesus—walking on the path of humanity, through the storm of Galilee, to the hill of Calvary. Jesus, the story of the God who came for us, died for us, rose for us. The story of the God who will come again.

His is the story that matters more than all the others.

B17 Flying Fortress

Eddie Rickenbacker

CHAPTER 1

A STORY OF SALVATION

John the Baptist saw a dove and believed. James Whittaker saw a seagull and believed. Who's to say the one who sent the first didn't send the second?

James Whittaker was a member of the handpicked crew that flew the B-17 Flying Fortress captained by Eddie Rickenbacker. Anybody who remembers October 1942 remembers the day Rickenbacker and his crew were reported lost at sea.

Somewhere over the Pacific, out of radio range, the plane ran out of fuel and crashed into the ocean. The nine men spent the next three weeks floating in three rafts. They battled the heat, the storms, and the water. Sharks, some ten feet long, would ram their nine-foot boats. After only eight days their rations were eaten or destroyed by salt water. It would take a miracle to survive.

Rickenbacker later said, "Throughout those twenty-one days of blistering sun and nights of ghastly chill, I never lost faith, and I felt that we were adrift for a purpose. I saw life had no meaning except in terms of helping others. I think man instinctively does not interest himself in others. He does it only by an act of will, when he sees that 'I am my brother's keeper' and 'Do unto others' are the essence of all truth. My experiences and the suffering through which I passed have taught me that faith in God is the answer to life."[1]

One morning after their daily devotions, Rickenbacker leaned his head back against the raft and pulled his hat over his eyes. A bird landed on his head. He peered out from under his hat. Every eye was on him. He instinctively knew it was a seagull.

Rickenbacker caught it, and the crew ate it. The bird's intestines were used for bait to catch fish . . . and the crew survived to tell the story. A story about a stranded crew with no hope or help in sight. A story about prayers offered and prayers answered. A story about a visitor from an unknown land traveling a great distance to give his life as a sacrifice.[2]

A story of salvation.

A story much like our own. Weren't we, like the crew, stranded? Weren't we, like the crew, praying? And weren't we, like the crew, rescued by a visitor we've never seen, through a sacrifice we'll never forget?

You may have heard the Rickenbacker story before. You may have even heard it from me. You may have read it in one of my books. Coreen did. She was engaged to the only crew member who did not survive, young Sgt. Alex Kaczmarczyk. As a result of a 1985 reunion of the crew, Mrs. Coreen Schwenk learned that the widow of crew member James Whittaker lived only eighty miles from her house. The two women met and shared their stories.

After reading this story in my book *In the Eye of the Storm*, Mrs. Schwenk felt compelled to write to me. The real miracle, she informed me, was not a bird on the head of Eddie Rickenbacker but a change in the heart of James Whittaker. The greatest event of that day was not the rescue of a crew but the rescue of a soul.

James Whittaker was an unbeliever. The plane crash didn't change his unbelief. The days facing death didn't cause him to reconsider his destiny. In fact, Mrs. Whittaker said her husband grew irritated with John Bartek, a crew member who continually read his Bible both privately and aloud.

But Whittaker's protests didn't stop Bartek from reading. Nor did Whittaker's resistance stop the Word from penetrating his soul. Unknown to Whittaker, the soil of his heart was being plowed. For it was one morning after a Bible reading that the seagull landed on Captain Rickenbacker's head.

And at that moment Jim became a believer.

I chuckled when I read the letter. Not at the letter; I believe every word of it. Nor at James Whittaker. I have every reason to believe his conversion was real. But I had to chuckle at . . . please excuse me . . . I had to chuckle at God.

Isn't that just like him? Who would go to such extremes to save a soul? Such an effort to get a guy's attention. The rest of the world is occupied with Germany and Hitler. Every headline is reporting the actions of Roosevelt and Churchill. The globe is locked in a battle for freedom . . . , and the Father is in the Pacific sending a missionary seagull to save a soul. Oh, the lengths to which God will go to get our attention and win our affection.

QUESTIONS FOR REFLECTION

Do you know someone who encountered God when he or she least expected it? Have you experienced that?

This story is filled with miracles. In your own life have you ever been blessed with a miracle within another miracle?

François Mauriac

Elie Wiesel

CHAPTER 2

OPEN MIND, OPEN HEART

E lie Wiesel was a correspondent for a Jewish newspaper in Paris, France, in 1954. A decade earlier he was a prisoner in a Jewish concentration camp. A decade later he would be known as the author of *Night*, an account of the Holocaust. Eventually he'll be awarded the Congressional Medal of Honor, Presidential Medal of Freedom, and the Nobel Peace Prize.

But tonight Elie Wiesel is a twenty-six-year-old unknown newspaper correspondent. He is about to interview the French author François Mauriac, who is a devout Christian. Mauriac is France's most recent Nobel laureate for literature and an expert on French political life.

Wiesel shows up at Mauriac's apartment, nervous and chain-smoking, his emotions still frayed from the German horror, his comfort as a writer still raw. The older Mauriac tries to put him at ease. He invites Wiesel in, and the two sit in the small room. Before Wiesel can ask a question, however, Mauriac, a staunch Roman Catholic, begins to speak about his favorite subject: Jesus. Wiesel grows uneasy. The name of Jesus is a pressed thumb on his infected wounds.

Wiesel tries to reroute the conversation but can't. It is as though everything in creation leads back to Jesus. Jerusalem? Jerusalem is where Jesus ministered. The Old Testament? Because of Jesus, the Old is now enriched by the New. Mauriac turns every topic toward the Messiah. The anger in Wiesel begins to heat up. The Christian anti-Semitism he'd grown up with, the layers of grief from Sighet, Auschwitz, and Buchenwald—it all boils over. He puts away his pen, shuts his notebook, and stands up angrily.

"Sir," he said to the still-seated Mauriac, "you speak of Christ. Christians love to speak of him. The passion of Christ, the agony of Christ, the death of Christ. In your religion, that is all you speak of. Well, I want you to know that ten years ago, not very far from here, I knew Jewish children every one of whom suffered a thousand times more, six million times more, than Christ on the cross. And we don't speak about them. Can you understand that, sir? We don't speak about them."[1]

Mauriac is stunned. Wiesel turns and marches out the door. Mauriac sits in shock, his woolen blanket still around him. The young reporter is pressing the elevator button when Mauriac appears in the hall. He gently reaches for Wiesel's arm. "Come back," he implores. Wiesel agrees, and the two sit on the sofa. At this point Mauriac begins to weep. He looks at Wiesel but says nothing. Just tears.

Wiesel starts to apologize. Mauriac will have nothing of it. Instead he urges his young friend to talk. He wants to hear about it—the camps, the trains, the deaths. He asks Wiesel why he hasn't put this to paper. Wiesel tells him the pain is too severe. He's made a vow of silence. The older man tells him to break it and speak out.

The evening changed them both. The drama became the soil of a lifelong friendship. They corresponded until Mauriac's death in 1970. Mauriac even dedicated a book on Jesus to him: "To Elie Wiesel, who was a crucified Jewish child."

"I owe François Mauriac my career," Wiesel said, and it was to Mauriac that Wiesel sent the first manuscript of *Night*.[2]

What if Mauriac had kept the door shut? Would anyone have blamed him? Cut by the sharp words of Wiesel, he could have become impatient with the angry young man and have been glad to be rid of him. But he didn't and he wasn't. He reacted decisively, quickly, and lovingly. He was "slow to boil." And because he was, a heart began to heal.

May I urge you to do the same?

"God is being patient with you" (2 Peter 3:9 ICB). And if God is being patient with you, can't you pass on some patience to others? Of course you can. Because before love is anything else, love is patient (1 Corinthians 13:4).

QUESTIONS FOR REFLECTION

Think about how patience and grace are related. How have patience and grace appeared in your life?

Patient love means choosing to love someone even when you don't feel like it or it isn't easy. When was the last time you've given or accepted patient love? How did love make the situation better?

CHAPTER 3

HUMBLE HEART

Esther Kim knows what true humility means. For thirteen years she had one dream. The Summer Olympics. She wanted to represent the United States on the Olympic Tae Kwon Do squad.

From the age of eight she spent every available hour in training. In fact, it was in training that she met and made her best friend, Kay Poe. Esther and Kay trained in Houston, coached by Esther's father, Jim Won Kim. They worked so hard for so long that no one was surprised when they both qualified for the 2000 Olympic trials in Colorado Springs.

Everyone, however, was surprised when they were placed in the same division. They'd never competed against each other, but when the number of divisions was reduced, they found their names on the same bracket. It would be just a matter of events before they found themselves on the same mat. One would win and one would lose. Only one could go to Sydney, Australia.

As if the moment needed more drama, two facts put Esther Kim in a heartrending position. First, her friend Kay dislocated her left kneecap in the match prior to theirs. Kay could scarcely walk, much

STORIES FOR YOUR SOUL

less compete. Because of the injury Esther could defeat her friend with hardly any effort.

But then there was a second truth. Esther knew that Kay was the better fighter. If she took advantage of her crippled friend, the better athlete would stay home.

So what did she do? Esther stepped onto the floor and bowed to her friend and opponent. Both knew the meaning of the gesture. Esther forfeited her place. She considered the cause more important than the credit.[1]

"I was in a very unfair situation. How can you go out there and fight someone who can't even stand up?" Esther said. "There was only one choice to be made, and that was just to forfeit and bow out."

"I felt blessed, and at the same time I almost felt, like, guilty," Kay said. "I couldn't express it any other way, but it just came out with my tears."[2]

True humility is not thinking lowly of yourself but thinking accurately of yourself. The humble heart does not say, "I can't do anything." But rather it says, "I can't do everything. I know my part and am happy to do it." The humble heart honors others.

QUESTIONS FOR REFLECTION

What is more important to you—that the work be done or that you be seen?

When someone is honored, are you joyful or jealous? Do you consider others more important than yourself?

Kathryn and Lewis Lawes

CHAPTER 4

THE ANGEL OF SING SING

Love never celebrates misfortune. Never. I like the way Eugene Peterson translates this passage: "Love . . . doesn't revel when others grovel, [but] takes pleasure in the flowering of truth" (1 Cor. 13:6 MSG). J. B. Phillips is equally descriptive: "Love . . . does not . . . gloat over the wickedness of other people. On the contrary, it is glad with all good men when truth prevails."

You know your love is real when you weep with those who weep and rejoice with those who rejoice. You know your love is real when you feel for others what Kathryn Lawes felt for the inmates of Sing Sing prison.

Sing Sing, formerly Ossining Correctional Facility, is a maximum-security prison operated by the New York State Department of Corrections and Community Supervision in Ossining, New York. The name "Sing Sing" was derived from the Sint Sink Native American tribe and is the former name of the surrounding town.

When Kathryn's husband, Lewis, became the warden in 1920, she was a young mother of three daughters. Everybody warned her never to step foot inside the walls. But she didn't listen to them. When the first prison basketball game was held, in she went, three girls in tow, and took a seat in the bleachers with the inmates.

She once said, "My husband and I are going to take care of these men, and I believe they will take care of me! I don't have to worry!"

When she heard that one convicted murderer was blind, she taught him braille so he could read. Upon learning of inmates who were hearing impaired, she studied sign language so they could communicate. For sixteen years Kathryn Lawes softened the hard hearts of the men of Sing Sing. In 1937 the world saw the difference real love makes.

The prisoners knew something was wrong when Lewis Lawes didn't report to work. Quickly the word spread that Kathryn had been killed in a car accident. The following day her body was placed in her home, three quarters of a mile from the prison. As the acting warden took his early morning walk, he noticed a large gathering at the main gate. Every prisoner against the fence. Eyes awash with tears. Faces solemn. No one spoke or moved. They'd come to stand as close as they could to the woman who'd given them love.

The warden made a remarkable decision. "All right, men, you can go. Just be sure to check in tonight." These were America's hardest criminals. Murderers. Robbers. These were men the nation had locked away for life. But the warden unlocked the gate for them, and they walked without escort or guard to the home of Kathryn Lawes to pay their last respects. And to a man, each one returned.[1]

Real love changes people.

QUESTIONS FOR REFLECTION

How would you define "real love"? Have you experienced it in your life?

Do you feel challenged to keep an open mind about a particular topic, person, or event? What can you do to soften your heart in this area?

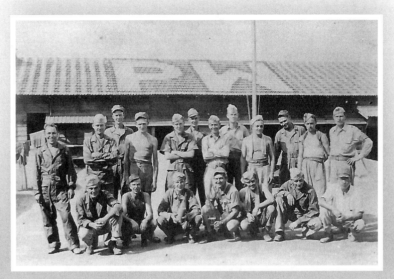

Arthur Bressi and other soldiers at Day of
Liberation from POW Camp

Arthur Bressi

CHAPTER 5

SOMEONE WORTH SAVING

B y all rules Skinner was a dead man." With these words Arthur Bressi begins his retelling of the day he found his best friend in a World War II Japanese concentration camp. The two were high-school buddies. They grew up together in Mount Carmel, Pennsylvania— playing ball, skipping school, double-dating. Arthur and Skinner were inseparable. It made sense, then, that when one joined the army, the other would as well. They rode the same troopship to the Philippines. That's where they were separated. Skinner was on Bataan when it fell to the Japanese in 1942. Arthur Bressi was captured a month later.

Through the prison grapevine, Arthur learned the whereabouts of his friend. Skinner was near death in a nearby camp. Arthur volunteered for work detail in the hope that his company might pass through the other camp. One day they did.

Arthur requested and was given five minutes to find and speak to his friend. He knew to go to the sick side of the camp. It was divided into two sections—one for those expected to recover, the other for those given no hope. Those expected to die lived in a barracks called "zero ward." That's where Arthur found Skinner. He called his name, and out of the barracks walked the seventy-nine-pound shadow of the friend he had once known.

As he writes:

> I stood at the wire fence of the Japanese prisoner-of-war camp on Luzon and watched my childhood buddy, caked in filth and racked with the pain of multiple diseases, totter toward me. He was dead; only his boisterous spirit hadn't left his body. I wanted to look away, but couldn't. His blue eyes, watery and dulled, locked on me and wouldn't let go.[1]

Malaria. Amoebic dysentery. Pellagra. Scurvy. Beriberi. Skinner's body was a dormitory for tropical diseases. He couldn't eat. He couldn't drink. He was nearly gone.

Arthur didn't know what to do or say. His five minutes were nearly up. He began to finger the heavy knot of the handkerchief tied around his neck. In it was his high-school class ring. At the risk of punishment, he'd smuggled the ring into camp. Knowing the imminence of disease and the scarcity of treatment, he had been saving it to barter for medicine or food for himself. But one look at Skinner, and he knew he couldn't save it any longer.

As he told his friend good-bye, he slipped the ring through the fence into Skinner's frail hand and told him to "wheel and deal" with it. Skinner objected, but Arthur insisted. He turned and left, not knowing if he would ever see his friend alive again.

Skinner buried the ring in the barracks floor. The next day he took the biggest risk of his life. He approached the "kindest" of the guards and passed him the ring through the fence. "*Takai?*" the guard asked. "Is it valuable?" Skinner assured him that it was. The guard smiled and slipped the ring into a pocket and left. A couple of days later he walked past Skinner and let a packet drop at his feet. Sulfanilamide tablets, used in that era to treat bacterial infections—this gave Skinner hope.

A day later the guard returned with limes to combat the scurvy. Then came a new pair of pants and some canned beef. Within three weeks Skinner was on his feet. Within three months he was taken to the healthy side of the sick camp. In time he was able to work. As far as Skinner knew, he was the only American ever to leave the zero ward alive.

All because of a ring. All because someone believed in him.

Arthur gave Skinner much more than a ring; he gave him a proclamation, a judgment that said, "You are worth this much to me! Your life is worth saving. Your life is worth living." He believed in him and, as a result, gave Skinner the means and the courage to save himself.

Both men returned home to Mount Carmel. One day soon after their arrival, Skinner came over for a visit. He had a gift with him. A small box. Arthur knew immediately what it was. It was an exact copy of the high-school ring. After a lame attempt at humor—"Don't lose that; it cost me eighteen dollars"—he gave his friend a warm smile and said, "That ring, Artie . . . it saved my life."[2]

QUESTIONS FOR REFLECTION

How can you show people that you believe in them? How could your presence make a difference for someone?

Has anyone showed you that you're worthy? If so, how did that change you?

Eddie O'Hare's car after being
tracked down by mobsters.

Edward "Butch" O'Hare

CHAPTER 6

A GANGSTER GONE GOOD

Artful Eddie lacked nothing. He was the slickest of the slick lawyers. He was one of the roars of the Roaring Twenties. A crony of Al Capone, he ran the gangster's dog tracks. He mastered the simple technique of fixing the race by overfeeding seven dogs and betting on the eighth.

Wealth. Status. Style. Artful Eddie lacked nothing.

Then why did he turn himself in? Why did he offer to squeal on Capone? What was his motive? Didn't Eddie know the surefire consequences of ratting on the mob?

He knew, but he'd made up his mind.

What did he have to gain? What could society give him that he didn't already have? He had money, power, prestige. What was the hitch?

Eddie revealed the hitch. His son. Eddie had spent his life with the despicable. He had smelled the stench of the underground long enough. For his son he wanted more. He wanted to give his son a name. And to give his son a name, he would have to clear his own.

Eddie was willing to take a risk so that his son could have a clean slate. Artful Eddie never saw his dream come true.

After Eddie squealed, the mob remembered. Two shotgun blasts silenced him forever.

Was it worth it?

For the son it was. Artful Eddie's boy lived up to the sacrifice. His is one of the best-known names in the world.

Had Eddie lived to see his son, Butch, grow up, he would have been proud.

He would have been proud of Butch's appointment to Annapolis. He would have been proud of the commissioning as a World War II navy pilot. He would have been proud as he read of his son downing five bombers in the Pacific night and saving the lives of hundreds of crewmen on the carrier *Lexington*. The name was cleared. The Congressional Medal of Honor that Butch received from President Roosevelt was proof.

When people say the name O'Hare in Chicago, they don't think gangsters. They think aviation heroism. And now when you say his name, you have something else to think about. Think about the undying dividends of risky love. Think about it the next time you hear it. Think about it the next time you fly into the airport named after the son of a gangster gone good.

The son of Eddie O'Hare.

QUESTIONS FOR REFLECTION

What would prompt you to exhibit risky love?

Has there been a situation in your life that called for risky love? What was the outcome?

CHAPTER 7

ANGELS AMONG US

E ric Hill had everything you'd need for a bright future. He was twenty-eight years old and a recent college grad with an athletic frame and a soft smile. His family loved him, girls took notice of him, and companies had contacted him about working for them. Although Eric appeared composed without, he was tormented within. Tormented by voices he could not still. Bothered by images he could not avoid. So, hoping to get away from them all, he got away from it all. On a gray, rainy day in February 1982, Eric Hill walked out the back door of his Florida home and never came back.

His sister Debbie remembers seeing him leave, his tall frame ambling down the interstate. She assumed he would return. He didn't. She hoped he would call. He didn't. She thought she could find him. She couldn't. Where Eric journeyed, only God and Eric know, and neither of them has chosen to tell. What we do know is Eric heard a voice. And in that voice was an "assignment." And that assignment was to pick up garbage along a roadside in San Antonio, Texas.

To the commuters on Interstate 10, his lanky form and bearded face became a familiar sight. He made a home out of a hole in a vacant lot. He made a wardrobe out of split trousers and a torn sweatshirt. An old hat deflected the summer sun. A plastic bag on his shoulders softened the winter chill. His weathered skin and stooped shoulders made him look twice his forty-four years. But then, sixteen years on the side of the road would do that to you.

That was how long it had been since Debbie had seen her brother. She might never have seen him again had it not been for two events. The first was the construction of a car dealership on Eric's vacant lot. The second was a severe pain in his abdomen. The dealership took his home. The pain nearly took his life.

EMS found him curled in a ball on the side of the road, clutching his stomach. The hospital ran some tests and found that Eric had cancer. Terminal cancer. Another few months and he would be dead. And with no known family or relatives, he would die alone.

His court-appointed attorney couldn't handle that thought. "Surely someone is looking for Eric," he reasoned. So the lawyer scoured the Internet for anyone in search of a brown-haired, adult male with the last name Hill. That's how he met Debbie.

His description seemed to match her memory, but she had to know for sure.

So Debbie came to Texas. She and her husband and two children rented a hotel room and set out to find Eric. By now he'd been released from the hospital, but the chaplain knew where he was. They found him sitting against a building not far from the interstate. As they approached, he stood. They offered fruit; he refused. They offered juice; he declined. He was polite but unimpressed with this family who claimed to be his own.

His interest perked, however, when Debbie offered him a pin to wear, an angel pin. He said yes. Her first time to touch her brother in sixteen years was the moment he allowed her to pin the angel on his shirt.

Debbie intended to spend a week. But a week passed, and she stayed. Her husband returned home, and she stayed. Spring became summer, and Eric improved, and still she stayed. Debbie rented an apartment and began homeschooling her kids and reaching out to her brother.

It wasn't easy. He didn't recognize her. He didn't know her. One day he cursed her. He didn't want to sleep in her apartment. He didn't want her food. He didn't want to talk. He wanted his vacant lot. He wanted his "job." Who was this woman anyway?

But Debbie didn't give up on Eric. She understood that he didn't understand. So she stayed.

I met her one Sunday when she visited our congregation. When she shared her story, I asked what you might want to ask. "How do you keep from giving up?"

"Simple," she said. "He's my brother."

Days before he died he recognized Debbie as his sister. And, in doing so, he discovered his true home.[1]

We will as well. Like Eric, we have doubted our Helper. But like Debbie, God has followed us on our journey. Like Eric, we are quick to turn away. But like Debbie, God is slow to anger and determined to stay. Like Eric, we don't accept God's gifts. But like Debbie, God still gives them. He gives us his angels, not just pinned on a lapel, but placed on our path.

QUESTIONS FOR REFLECTION

Who, in your life, would you never give up on? How can you show them that they matter?

Do you have an "angel" who stood by you during a difficult time? How did this person impact your life?

CHAPTER 8

EAGLES OVER WOLVES

Nadin Khoury was thirteen years old, five foot two, and weighed, soaking wet, probably a hundred pounds.

His attackers were teenagers, larger than Nadin, and out numbered him seven to one.

For thirty minutes they hit, kicked, and beat him.

He was just trying to walk home from school. He never stood a chance. Nadin's mom had recently moved the family to Philadelphia from Minnesota. She had lost her job as a hotel maid and was looking for work. In 2000 she'd escaped war-torn Liberia. Nadin Khoury, then, was the new kid in a rough neighborhood with a mom who was an unemployed immigrant—everything a wolf pack of bullies needed to justify an attack.

The hazing had begun weeks earlier. They picked on him. They called his mother names. They routinely pushed, shoved, and ambushed him. Then came the all-out assault on a January day. They dragged him through the snow, stuffed him into a tree, and then suspended him on a seven-foot wrought-iron fence.

Nadin survived the attack and would have likely faced a few more except for the folly of one of the bullies. He filmed the pile on and posted it on YouTube. A passerby saw the violence and chased away the bullies. Police saw it and got involved. The troublemakers landed in jail, and the story reached the papers.

A staffer at the nationwide morning show *The View* read the account and invited Nadin to appear on the broadcast. He did. As the video of the assault played on the screen behind him, he tried to appear brave, but his lower lip quivered. "Next time maybe it could be somebody smaller than me," he said.

Unbeknown to him the producer had invited some other Philadelphians to appear on the show as well. As the YouTube video ended, the curtain opened, and three huge men walked out, members of the Philadelphia Eagles football team—DeSean Jackson, Jamaal Jackson, and Todd Herremans.

Nadin, a rabid fan, turned and smiled. All-Pro receiver DeSean Jackson was Nadin's favorite player. Jackson took a seat on the couch as close to the boy as possible and promised him, "Anytime you need us, I got two linemen right here." Nadin's eyes widened saucer-like as Jackson signed a football jersey and handed it to him. Then, in full view of every bully in America, he gave the boy his cell phone number.[1]

From that day forward Nadin has been only a call away from his personal bodyguards. Criminals think twice before they harass the kid who has an NFL football player's number on speed dial. Pretty good offer.

QUESTIONS FOR REFLECTION

Have you ever been bullied? Did anyone come to your rescue?

In what ways have unexpected protectors stood up for you?
In what ways have you stood up for someone being bullied?

CHAPTER 9

RECYCLED HOPE

S ome kids in Cateura, on the outskirts of Asunción, Paraguay, are making music with their trash. They're turning washtubs into kettledrums and drainpipes into trumpets. Other orchestras fine-tune their maple cellos or brass tubas. Not this band. They play Beethoven sonatas with plastic buckets.

On their side of Asunción, garbage is the only crop to harvest. Garbage pickers sort and sell refuse for pennies a pound. Many of them have met the same fate as the trash; they've been tossed out and discarded.

But now, thanks to two men, they are making music.

Favio Chavez is an environmental technician who envisioned a music school as a welcome reprieve for the kids. Don Cola Gomez is a trash worker and carpenter. He had never seen, heard, or held a violin in his life. Yet when someone described the instrument, this untutored craftsman took a paint can and an oven tray into his tiny workshop and made a violin. His next instrument was a cello. He fashioned the body out of an oil barrel and made tuning knobs from a hairbrush, the heel of a shoe, and a wooden spoon.

"The world gives us trash; we give them back music," said Favio.

Thanks to this newfangled "Stradivarius," the junk gets a mulligan, and so do the kids who live among it. Since the day their story hit the news, they've been tutored by maestros, featured on national television programs, and taken on a world tour. They've been called the Landfill Harmonic and also the Recycled Orchestra of Cateura.[1]

We could also call them a picture of God's grace.

By taking the world's trash and giving back music, Favio and Don Cola aim not only to raise public awareness of a global issue but also to demonstrate that, despite extreme poverty, students can become contributing members of the community.

God makes music out of the unlikely. Heaven's orchestra is composed of the unlikeliest of musicians. Peter, first-chair trumpeter, cursed the name of the Christ, who saved him. Paul plays the violin. But there was a day when he played the religious thug. And the guy on the harp? That's David. King David. Womanizing David. Conniving David. Bloodthirsty David. Repentant David.

Ultimately we all will see what the people of Asunción are discovering. Our mess will become music—that'll be me on the tuba. And you? What will you be playing? One thing is for sure. We will all know "Amazing Grace" by heart.

QUESTIONS FOR REFLECTION

The Landfill Harmonic and the Recycled Orchestra of Cateura is a picture of God's grace. Can you think of an example of God's grace in your own community?

Why do you think God leans into the most unlikely situations and people to make beautiful things?

Jimmy Wayne Barber

Jimmy Wayne Barber speaking to an audience

CHAPTER 10

UNPACK YOUR BAGS

Jimmy Wayne Barber never knew his father. His mom spent more time in prison than out. When he was twelve years old, she was released from jail and took up with a troublemaker. They loaded Jimmy into the backseat of the Oldsmobile Delta 88, and for a year the car was their home. "It had bench seats and smelled like body odor," remembers Jimmy. They drove from city to city, avoiding the police.

After miles of drifting they dumped Jimmy in the parking lot of a Pensacola, Florida, bus station and drove off. He was thirteen years old. He had no home. No future. No provision. One day while wandering through a neighborhood, he spotted an older man who was at work in a garage wood shop.

He approached the elderly gentleman and asked the man if he had any work. The carpenter sized up the boy, assessed him to be homeless, and decided to give him a chance. The man introduced himself as Russell Costner. He called for his wife, Bea, to come to the garage. They showed Jimmy the lawn mower and how to operate it.

For several weeks Jimmy cut the couple's grass and survived on the twenty dollars they paid him each week. After some time Bea asked Jimmy where he lived. At first he lied, afraid she wouldn't let a homeless boy work. But finally she convinced him to tell her the truth. When he did, the couple took him in.

They gave him his own bedroom, bathroom, and place at the dinner table. The home was like heaven to Jimmy. He took a hot bath and ate hot meals. He even sat with the family in the living room and watched television in the evening. Still, in spite of their kindness, Jimmy refused to unpack his bag. He'd been turned away so many times that he'd learned to be wary. For four days his plastic bag sat on the floor, full of clothes, ready to be snatched up when Bea and Russell changed their minds.

He was in the house but not *in* the house. He was under the roof but not under the promise. He was with the family but didn't behave like a family member.

Russell eventually convinced Jimmy to unpack and move in. It took several days, a dozen or so meals, and more than one heart-to-heart conversation. But Russell persuaded Jimmy to trust them to care for him.[1]

Our Father is still working to convince us.

Maybe you question your place in God's family. You fear his impending rejection. You wrestle with doubt-laced questions: Am I really in God's family? What if God changes his mind? Reverses his acceptance? Lord knows, he has reason to do so. We press forward only to fall back. We renew our resolve only to stumble again. We wonder, *Will God turn me out?*

Boyfriends do. Employers do. Coaches kick players off the team.

Teachers expel students from school. Parents give birth to children and abandon them at bus stations. How do we know God won't do the same? What if he changes his mind about us? After all, he is holy and pure, and we are anything but. Is it safe to unpack our bags?

God answered this question at the cross. When Jesus died, the heavenly vote was forever cast in your favor and mine. He declared for all to hear, "This child is my child. My covenant will never change."

Those who know Jesus trust God's hold on them more than their hold on God. They place their trust in the finished work of Christ. They deeply believe that they are "delivered . . . from the power of darkness and conveyed . . . into the kingdom of the Son" (Col. 1:13 NKJV). They know that Jesus was serious when he said, "[My children] shall never perish; no one will snatch them out of my hand" (John 10:28 NIV).

Rest in your redemption. The past is past. The future is bright. God's Word is sure. His work is finished. You are a covenant partner with God, a full-fledged member of his Promised Land development program.

A new season awaits you.

Jimmy Wayne found a new season. He took his place in the family. He went on to graduate high school, earn a degree in criminal justice, and work as a corrections officer for four years before moving to Nashville, Tennessee. There he found a career as a country music singer, songwriter, and inspirational speaker.

QUESTIONS FOR REFLECTION

Jimmy's story relies heavily on trust. Trust in God's plan is simple, but sometimes it is hard to be faithful in the unknown. Have you experienced a moment or season when you felt abandoned and lost? Who came to your aid? How did God lead you to a new season?

Max says our Father is still working to convince us to trust him. What can you do to deepen your trust in our Father?

Tammy Trent

CHAPTER 11

COMFORTED BY A STRANGER

ammy Trent and her husband, Trent Lenderink, went to Jamaica shortly after their eleventh wedding anniversary. They enjoyed some wonderful island time, and as they were leaving the area, Trent decided to stop and check out the blue lagoon, a favorite diving spot on the island. He suited up: wet suit, mask, fins, underwater scooter. Trent's plan was to swim in the blue lagoon for about fifteen minutes. Tammy waited at the water's edge, eating lunch, watching Trent resurface for air every few minutes. Then she realized she hadn't seen him for a while. Tammy says, "I began to fight back fear when he didn't appear after thirty minutes and then forty-five minutes."

A dive team went to look for Trent. The search continued until night fell and then resumed the next morning, September 11, 2001. Tammy watched the news as the second plane plowed into the twin towers in New York City. Moments later a call from the dock confirmed that Trent had been found. He had drowned in the lagoon.

Tammy was in shock. The two had been sweethearts since high school. Now she was all alone in a foreign country. She called her parents. All flights were grounded. Tammy's parents could not come to her. She could not leave Jamaica. A couple of days later Tammy made her way to Kingston, where she and Trent had planned to begin a mission trip. There, alone in a hotel room, Tammy came undone. *God,* she prayed, *if you are up there anywhere, please send somebody to help me, somebody to hold me and let me know that you care and that you see me.*

A few minutes later there was a knock at her hotel door. It was the housekeeper. She was an older Jamaican woman. "I don't mean to bother you," she said, "but I couldn't help but hear you crying, and I was trying to get to you. Could I just come in and hold you and pray for you?"

Tammy broke down in tears. She told the woman what had happened. That kind Jamaican put her arms around Tammy and held her close.

Jesus used a Jamaican housekeeper to comfort his American daughter.[1]

God had used a stranger to remind her of his presence, even in the darkest of times.

Look to Jesus to comfort you. Healing happens when we look to him. And worship the compassionate healer. Lift up your eyes and bow your knees.

Sometime later Tammy reflected on what her personal tragedy had taught her. "There is hope," she said. "There is hope. There is future. God's got a bigger plan than any of us know. He's not surprised by any of this . . . My hope has been built on Jesus Christ . . . In times like this my faith and trust in the Lord is somewhat being tested . . . What do I believe? Where is my hope? Where is my faith?

I know I will see Trent again, but it is only because of my relationship with Jesus Christ."

QUESTIONS FOR REFLECTION

Have you experienced surprising compassion when you desperately needed it?

Where do you place your faith? In unexpected challenges, where do you turn for hope?

Taylor Storch

The Storch Family

CHAPTER 12

GRIEF AND GRATEFULNESS

Tara and Todd Storch understand the real meaning of grace. Grace comes after us. It rewires us. Grace is the voice that calls us to change and then gives us the power to pull it off.[1]

In the spring of 2010 a skiing accident took the life of their thirteen-year-old daughter, Taylor. It was the family's last day on the slopes when Taylor lost control and slammed into a tree. What followed was every parent's worst nightmare: a funeral, a burial, a flood of questions and tears. Todd said, "We went from it being the most amazing trip ever to the worst nightmare."[2] They decided to donate their daughter's organs to needy patients. Few people needed a heart more than Patricia Winters, a labor and delivery nurse and mom of two. Her heart had begun to fail five years earlier, leaving her too weak to do much more than sleep. Tara and Todd donated Taylor's heart to Patricia and provided her with a fresh start on life.

"When faced with that decision, we knew it was the right choice for our family. But also we knew it would be something Taylor would have chosen," said Tara.[3]

Tara had only one request: she wanted to hear the heart of her daughter. Six months after Taylor's death, she and Todd flew from Dallas to Phoenix and went to Patricia's home to listen to Taylor's heart.

The two mothers embraced for a long time. Then Patricia offered Tara and Todd a stethoscope.[4] When they listened to the healthy rhythm, whose heart did they hear? Did they not hear the still-beating heart of their daughter? It indwells a different body, but the heart is the heart of their child.

Later Tara and Todd founded Taylor's Place at Southwest Transplant Alliance in Dallas, Texas. It is a place where grief and gratefulness share the same space. The facility serves as a home and safe place for organ donor families who are grieving in the hospital and trying to emotionally navigate the sudden loss of their loved one. "We're able to make the world a little bit better than we found it, so we have to be grateful for that," said Todd.[5]

Tara continues to share her message of hope and inspiration. She challenges others to think differently, to overcome their own obstacles, no matter how big or small, and to turn them into something impactful, something that can make a difference in the lives of others. Tara shares, "It's not what happens to you that matters; it's how you react to it that does."[6]

QUESTIONS FOR REFLECTION

Have you received or given grace that calls for change?

How can you embody the message of grace in your life?

CHAPTER 13

UNFATHOMABLE
FORGIVENESS

People bring pain. Sometimes deliberately. Sometimes randomly. Victoria Ruvolo can tell you about random pain. On a November evening in 2004, this New Yorker was driving to her home in Ronkonkoma, New York, on Long Island. She'd just attended her niece's recital. Her friend Louis Erali was in the passenger seat of her Hyundai.

She doesn't remember seeing the silver Nissan approach from the east. She remembers nothing of Ryan, the eighteen-year-old boy leaning out the window holding, of all things, a frozen turkey. He threw it at her windshield.

The twenty-pound bird crashed through the glass, bent the steering wheel inward, and shattered her face. Louis pulled Victoria's foot from the gas pedal, steered the damaged car to a stop, and cradled her head until an ambulance arrived. The violent prank left her grappling for life in the ICU. Victoria's bones in her cheeks and jaw were crushed. Her left eye socket was fractured, causing her esophagus to cave in and leaving her with brain trauma.

She survived but only after doctors wired her jaw, affixed one eye by synthetic film, and bolted titanium plates to her cranium. She underwent physical and cognitive rehabilitation for months.

"Once I got off the medication, I remember lying in the bedroom at my sister's house and just crying myself to sleep and asking: Why me God? What did I ever do so wrong and so terrible in my life that I deserved all this to happen to me? And I'd cry myself to sleep. But then gradually it began to dawn on me that perhaps God had allowed me to live through this ordeal because I was in such great physical condition. The idea it had happened for a reason—and that I had saved someone else who might not have been able to survive—helped me get through rehabilitation."[1]

The Suffolk County prosecutors wanted to charge the eighteen-year-old boy with the maximum of twenty-five years in prison for first-degree assault and several other offenses. But Victoria argued that a long sentence, like the prosecutors were pursuing, would only turn the young boy into a hardened criminal. She wanted to offer him grace and forgiveness. Victoria publicly pleaded for a shorter sentence for the boy and met with Ryan's lawyer to tell him that she wanted amnesty for Ryan or at least a lesser sentence.

Instead of being enraged with bitterness and anger, Victoria wanted answers. Had Ryan been bullied? Was he hurting other people? Victoria had experienced the death of her two brothers when she was younger, so she didn't want to be responsible for taking another young person's life and allowing him to rot in jail.

After a guilty plea in August 2005, Ryan was sentenced to six months in prison and five years of probation. At his sentencing he told Victoria, "Your ability to forgive has had a profound effect on me. It has already made a positive change in my life."[2] Victoria requested that Ryan "do something good with his life, take this experience, and do something good in his life."

The compassion and forgiveness that Victoria gave a complete stranger is unfathomable. Her decision not to default to vengeance was powerful and changed the trajectory of a troubled boy's life.

QUESTIONS FOR REFLECTION

Consider a time you were on the receiving end of forgiveness. In what ways did it change you?

Consider a time you gave forgiveness. How did you come to that decision? How was it received?

Amy Wells

CHAPTER 14

A SIMPLE ACT OF KINDNESS

Amy Wells knew her bridal shop would be busy. Brides-to-be took full advantage of the days right after Thanksgiving. It was common for a cluster of in-laws and siblings to spend the better part of the holiday weekend looking at wedding dresses in her San Antonio, Texas, store. Amy was prepared to give service to the shoppers. She never expected she would be giving grace to a dying man.

Across town Jack Autry was in the hospital, struggling to stay alive. He was in the final stages of melanoma. He had collapsed two days before and had been rushed to the emergency room. His extended family was in town not just to celebrate Thanksgiving together but to make preparations for his daughter's wedding. Chrysalis was only months from marriage. The women in the family had planned to spend the day selecting a wedding gown. But now with Jack in the hospital, Chrysalis didn't want to go.

Jack insisted. After much persuasion Chrysalis, her mother, her future mother-in-law, and her sisters went to the bridal salon. Amy, the shop owner, noticed that the women were a bit subdued, but she assumed this was just a quiet family. She helped Chrysalis try on dress after dress until she found an ivory duchess silk and satin gown that everyone loved. Jack was fond of calling Chrysalis his princess, and the dress, Chrysalis commented, made her look just like one.

That's when Amy heard about Jack. Because of the cancer, he couldn't come see his daughter in her dress. And because of the medical bills, the family couldn't buy the dress yet. It appeared that Jack Autry would die without seeing his daughter dressed as a bride.

Amy would hear nothing of it. She told Chrysalis to take the gown and veil to the hospital and wear it for her daddy. She says, "I knew it was fine. There was no doubt in my mind to do this. God was talking to me." No credit card was requested or given. Amy didn't even make note of a phone number. She urged the family to go directly to the hospital. Chrysalis didn't have to be told twice.

When she arrived at her father's room, he was heavily medicated and asleep. As family members woke him, the doors to the room slowly opened, and there he saw his daughter, engulfed in fifteen yards of layered, billowing silk. He was able to stay alert for about twenty seconds.

"But those twenty seconds were magical," Chrysalis remembers. "My daddy saw me walk in wearing the most beautiful dress. He was really weak. He smiled and just kept looking at me. I held his hand, and he held mine. I asked him if I looked like a princess . . . He nodded. He looked at me a little more, and it almost seemed as if he was about to cry. And then he went to sleep."

Three days later he died.[1]

Amy's simple kindness created a special memory that Chrysalis and her family will retell and cherish. "This woman had never met me before. She trusted me and showed me that there are still some really good people out there, special people in this world," Chrysalis says about Amy's compassion. "It's every little girl's dream to have her dad see her in a wedding dress. She let my dad and me have that amazing moment."[2]

QUESTIONS FOR REFLECTION

What do you consider to be the connection between grace and generosity? Describe your reaction when you see grace happening around you.

What simple acts of kindness have left lifelong impressions on you?

Mount Everest

Dan Mazur skiing

CHAPTER 15

AMBITION SURRENDERED

D an Mazur considered himself lucky. Most people would have considered him crazy. He stood within a two-hour hike of the summit of Mount Everest, a thousand feet from realizing a lifelong dream.

Every year the fittest adventurers on earth set their sights on the twenty-nine-thousand–foot peak. Every year some die in the effort. The top of Everest isn't known for its hospitality. Climbers call the realm above twenty-six thousand feet "the death zone."

Temperatures hover below zero. Sudden blizzards stir blinding snow. The atmosphere is oxygen starved. Corpses dot the mountaintop. A British climber had died ten days prior to Mazur's attempt. Forty climbers who could have helped chose not to do so. They passed him on the way to the summit.

Everest can be cruel.

Still, Mazur felt lucky. He and two colleagues were within eyesight of the top. Years of planning. Six weeks of climbing, and now at 7:30 A.M., May 25, 2006, the air was still, morning sun brilliant, energy and hopes high.

That's when a flash of color caught Mazur's eye: a bit of yellow fabric on the ridgetop. He first thought it was a tent. He soon saw it was a person, a man precariously perched on an eight-thousand-foot razor-edge rock. His gloves were off, jacket unzipped, hands exposed, chest bare. Oxygen deprivation can swell the brain and stir hallucinations. Mazur knew this man had no idea where he was, so he walked toward him and called out.

"Can you tell me your name?"

"Yes," the man answered, sounding pleased. "I can. My name is Lincoln Hall."

Mazur was shocked. He recognized this name. Twelve hours earlier he'd heard the news on the radio: "Lincoln Hall is dead on the mountain. His team has left his body on the slope."

And yet, after spending the night in twenty-below chill and oxygen-stingy air, Lincoln Hall was still alive. Mazur was face-to-face with a miracle.

He was also face-to-face with a choice. A rescue attempt had profound risks. The descent was already treacherous, even more so with the dead weight of a dying man. Besides, how long would Hall survive? No one knew. The three climbers might sacrifice their Everest for naught. They had to choose: abandon their dream or abandon Lincoln Hall.

They chose to abandon their dream. The three turned their backs on the peak and inched their way down the mountain.[1]

Lincoln Hall survived the trip down Mount Everest. Thanks to Dan Mazur, he lived to be reunited with his wife and sons in New Zealand. A television reporter asked Lincoln's wife what she thought of the rescuers, the men who surrendered their summit to save her husband's life. She tried to answer, but the words stuck in her throat. After several moments and with tear-filled eyes, she offered, "Well, there's one amazing human being. And the other men with him. The world needs more people like that."[2]

QUESTIONS FOR REFLECTION

Would you surrender ambition to save someone else? Set aside your dreams to help someone?

What emotions do you experience when you help someone?

Kayla Montgomery

CHAPTER 16

I GOT YOU

Ask those who watched Kayla Montgomery run, and they will tell you that Kayla was a steady runner, a sturdy runner. Whip thin and determined, she was one of the fastest long- distance racers in the country. Trained eyes took note of her stride and strong finish. Her performance on the high school squad in Winston-Salem, North Carolina, caught the attention of coaches, competitors, and colleges. She set distance records, won state titles, competed in nationals, and eventually landed an athletic scholarship to Lipscomb University in Nashville, Tennessee.

Had you watched her run, you would have been impressed.

Here is what you never would have imagined: she ran with no feeling in her legs. She was diagnosed with multiple sclerosis at the age of fifteen. The disease is an autoimmune disorder that strictly targets the myelin sheath of the nerves, affecting the brain and spine. Heat sensitivity is one of many possible symptoms of MS. When Kayla overheats, her MS symptoms flare up, leaving her numb from the waist down. "My initial MS attack caused lesions and scarring on my brain and my spine that affects the areas that are in control of how I feel my legs. So when I am overheated the symptoms reappear because my neurons start misfiring more," Kayla said.[1]

Still she wanted to run. She told her coach, "I want to run, and I want to run fast." And she did. At one time she was ranked twenty-first in the nation.

The numbness would begin to set in after the first-mile marker. After that she relied on the momentum, as if on autopilot, to keep moving. Running was doable. Stopping? That was another story. She would cross the finish line with no ability to decelerate.

For this she depended entirely on one man, Patrick Cromwell, her coach. He was a fixture at the races, shouting, encouraging, and prodding, but his greatest contribution was catching. He caught Kayla. He would stand at the finish line awaiting her. She ran right into his arms. She didn't slow down. He didn't move. It was no small collision. When he finally was able to halt her forward progress, he would lift her five-feet-one-inch frame in a heap and carry her off the track.

Over and over she could be heard saying, "My legs! My legs! Where'd they go? Please help me. Please help me."

Over and over the coach assured, "It's okay. I got you. I got you."

He would carry her to a safe spot and give her water and ice. Gradually her body temperature would lower, and the feeling in her legs would return.[2]

They had an agreement. She did the running; he did the catching. If he was not present to catch her, she would eventually crash into the next obstacle. But she never crashed, because he was ever-present.

This was his pledge to her.

This is God's pledge to us.

Your finish line is drawing near. Each beat of the heart is the click of a countdown clock. No matter how well you run this race, you will not run it forever. You're going to need some help.

You're going to need someone to catch you.

Jesus has promised to be that Someone. He will not abandon you in your final moments. This is his promise.

Keep running the race. And as you run, be assured. A Friend is waiting for you at the finish line. When you cross it, he'll catch you in his arms. Don't be surprised if he says again what he said then: "It is finished."

QUESTIONS FOR REFLECTION

Who is the Coach Cromwell in your race of life?

In what ways has the encouragement of others made a difference in your life?

CHAPTER 17

QUIET GIVERS

M any recipients of an act of kindness don't know the person behind the action, but they are grateful for the regular people who want to leave the world a little bit better than they found it.

Edith Hayes was a spry eighty-year-old with thinning white hair, a wiry five-foot frame, and an unquenchable compassion for South Florida's cancer patients.

Her team included a hundred or so silver-haired women who occupied themselves with the unglamorous concern of sore seepage. They made cancer wounds their mission, stitching together truckloads of disposable pads each Tuesday, then delivering them to patients throughout the week.

Edith rented an alley apartment, lived on her late husband's pension, wore glasses that magnified her pupils, and ducked applause like artillery fire.

So do Joe and Liz Page. Their battalion has a different objective— clothing for premature infants. They turn one of our church classrooms into a factory of volunteer seamstresses. The need for doll-sized wardrobes had never occurred to me. But then again, my children weren't born weighing only three pounds. Joe and Liz make sure such kids have something to wear, even if they wear it to their own funerals.

Joe retired from military service. Liz once taught school. He has heart problems. She has foot deformities. But both have a fire in their hearts for the neediest of children.

As does Caleb. He's nine years old. He plays basketball, avoids girls, and wants the kids of El Salvador to have clean drinking water.

During a Sunday school class, his teacher shared the reality of life in poverty-stricken Central America. For lack of clean drinking water, children die every day of preventable diseases. Caleb was stunned at the thought and stepped into action. He took the twenty dollars he had been saving for a new video game, gave it to the cause, and asked his father to match it. He then challenged the entire staff of the children's ministry at his church to follow his example. The result? Enough money to dig two wells in El Salvador.

Edith, Joe, Liz, and Caleb are regular folks. They don't levitate when they walk or see angels when they pray. They don't have a seat at the United Nations or a solution for the suffering in Darfur. But they do embrace this conviction: God doesn't call the qualified. He qualifies the called.

QUESTIONS FOR REFLECTION

Think about someone who did something ordinary for you, but it made an extraordinary difference. What small thing could you do that would have a big impact?

What act of kindness have you received from someone you never met?

Nicholas Winton as a young adult

Nicholas Winton visiting Prague in October 2007

CHAPTER 18

A HEART FOR THE CHILDREN

A re you more dinghy than cruise ship? More stand-in than movie star? More plumber than executive? More blue jeans than blue blood? Congratulations. God changes the world with people like you.

Just ask the twenty-two people who traveled to London on a fall morning in 2009 to thank Nicholas Winton. They could have passed for a retirement-home social club. All were in their seventies or eighties. More gray hair than not. More shuffled steps than quick ones.

But this was no social trip. It was a journey of gratitude. They came to thank the man who had saved their lives: a stooped centenarian who met them on a train platform just as he had in 1939.

He was a twenty-nine-year-old stockbroker at the time. Hitler's armies were ravaging the nation of Czechoslovakia, tearing Jewish families apart, and marching parents to concentration camps. No one was caring for the children. Winton got wind of their plight and resolved to help them. His motto was, "If something is not impossible, then there must be a way to do it."[1] He used his vacation to travel to Prague, where he met parents who, incredibly, were willing to entrust their children's future to his care. After returning to England, he worked his regular job on the stock exchange by day and advocated for the children at night. He convinced Great Britain to permit their entry. He found foster homes and raised funds. Then he scheduled his first transport on March 14, 1939, and accomplished seven more over the next five months. His last trainload of children arrived on August 2, bringing the total of rescued children to 669.

On September 1 the biggest transport was to take place, but Hitler invaded Poland, and Germany closed borders throughout Europe. None of the 250 children on that train were ever seen again.

After the war Winton didn't tell anyone, not even his wife, of his rescue efforts. In 1988 she found a scrapbook in their attic with all the children's photos and a complete list of names. She prodded him to tell the story. As he has, rescued children have returned to say thank you. The grateful group includes a film director, a Canadian journalist, a news correspondent, a former minister in the British cabinet, a magazine manager, and one of the founders of the Israeli Air Force. There are some six thousand children, grandchildren, and great-grandchildren who owe their existence to Winton's bravery. He wears a ring given to him by some of the children he saved. It bears a line from the Talmud, the book of Jewish law: "Save one life. Save the world."[2]

QUESTIONS FOR REFLECTION

Can you think of an event in your life that positively affected other people? How did it change the future for those people?

Describe one way God has used you to "rescue" someone.

Coach Kris Hogan

CHAPTER 19

MORE THAN A GAME

Fans rooted for the competition. Cheerleaders switched loyalties. The coach helped the opposition score points. Parents yelled for the opposing team.

What was this?

This was the brainchild of a big-hearted football coach in Grapevine, Texas. Kris Hogan ran the successful program of Faith Christian High School. He had seventy players, eleven coaches, quality equipment, and parents who cared, made banners, attended pep rallies, and wouldn't miss a game for their own funeral.

They took their 7–2 record into a contest with Gainesville State School. Gainesville's players, by contrast, wore seven-year-old shoulder pads and last decade's helmets and showed up at each game wearing handcuffs. Their parents didn't watch them play, but twelve uniformed officers did. That's because Gainesville is a maximum-security correctional facility for boys twelve to nineteen years old. The school doesn't have a stadium, cheerleading squad, or half a hope of winning. Gainesville was 0–8 going into the Grapevine game. They'd scored two touchdowns all year. At Gainesville the boys who are juniors and seniors have to earn the right to play. They must have served half their sentence, have no behavioral incidents, and maintain good grades.

The whole situation didn't seem fair. So Coach Hogan devised a plan. He asked the fans to step across the field and, for one night only, to cheer for the other side. More than two hundred volunteered.

"I told them that we had an opportunity. I wanted to send a message to these Gainesville kids that they are just as important and valuable as any other kid on planet Earth. We wanted to show them that Jesus loves them and we love them," Coach Hogan said. "And I wanted to affirm their good choices for them having earned the right to play football."[1]

They formed a forty-yard spirit line. They painted "Go Tornadoes!" on a banner that the Gainesville squad could burst through. They sat on the Gainesville side of the stadium. They even learned the names of the Gainesville players so they could cheer for them.

The prisoners had heard people scream their names but never like this. Gerald, a lineman who will serve three years, said, "People are a little afraid of us when we come to the games. You can see it in their eyes. They're lookin' at us like we're criminals. But these people, they were yellin' for us. By our names!"

"They had no idea what to do. They sprinted through the spirit line and were pumped up. They acted like they just played in the Super Bowl because people were loving on them," Coach Hogan said.

Faith beat Gainesville 33–14. The Gainesville squad was so happy that after the game they gave their head coach, Mark Williams, a sideline squirt of Gatorade.

After the game the teams gathered in the middle of the field to say a prayer. One of the incarcerated players asked to lead it. Coach Hogan agreed, not knowing what to expect. "Lord," the boy said, "I don't know how this happened, so I don't know how to say thank you, but I never would've known there was so many people in the world that cared about us."

Grapevine fans weren't finished. After the game they waited beside the Gainesville bus to give each player a good-bye gift—burger, fries, candy, soda, a Bible, an encouraging letter, and a round of applause. As their bus left the parking lot, the players pressed stunned faces against the windows and wondered what had just hit them.[2]

QUESTIONS FOR REFLECTION

Do any walls bisect your world? What are the root causes? What prevents the walls from coming down?

How could you tell a person on the other side of the wall that he or she matters to you? What could you do to show that person you care?

Sam Brown

CHAPTER 20

NEW DREAMS

Two years out of West Point, Lieutenant Sam Brown was on his first tour of duty in Afghanistan when an improvised explosive device turned his Humvee into a Molotov cocktail. He doesn't remember how he got out of the truck. He does remember rolling in the sand, slapping dirt on his burning face, running in circles, and finally dropping to his knees. He lifted flaming arms to the air and cried, "Jesus, save me!"

In Sam's case the words were more than a desperate scream. He is a devoted believer in Jesus Christ. Sam was calling on his Savior to take him home. He assumed he would die.

But death did not come. His gunner did. With bullets flying around them, he helped Sam reach cover. Crouching behind a wall, Sam realized that bits of his clothing were fusing to his skin. He ordered the private to rip his gloves off the burning flesh. The soldier hesitated, then pulled. With the gloves came pieces of his hands. Brown winced at what was the first of thousands of moments of pain.

When vehicles from another platoon reached them, they loaded the wounded soldier into a truck. Before Sam passed out, he caught a glimpse of his singed face in the mirror. He didn't recognize himself.

That was September 2008. By the time I met him three years later, he had undergone dozens of painful surgeries. Dead skin had been excised and healthy skin harvested and grafted. The pain chart didn't have a number high enough to register the agony he felt. He suffered third degree burns on 30 percent of his body—mostly in the places his body armor didn't cover. He also lost his left index finger.

Yet in the midst of the horror, beauty walked in. Dietitian Amy Larsen. Since Sam's mouth had been reduced to the size of a coin and burn victims tend to have fluctuating weight gain after their injuries, Amy monitored his nutrition intake. He remembers the first time he saw her. Dark hair, brown eyes. Nervous. Cute. More important, she didn't flinch at the sight of him.

"I had plans for my career and decided a few years after that I would find a beautiful woman and settle down and start a family," Sam said. "I thought that was all gone after I got injured."[1]

After several weeks he gathered the courage to ask her out. They went to a rodeo. The following weekend they went to a friend's wedding. During the three-hour drive Amy told Sam how she had noticed him months earlier when he was in ICU, covered with bandages, sedated with morphine, and attached to a breathing machine. When he regained consciousness, she stepped into his room to meet him. But there was a circle of family and doctors, so she turned and left.

The two continued to see each other. Early in their relationship Sam brought up the name Jesus Christ. Amy was not a believer. Sam's story stirred her heart for God. Sam talked to her about God's mercy and led her to Christ. Soon thereafter they were married. They grew their family, welcoming two boys and a girl. Now Sam and Amy direct a program to aid wounded soldiers.[2] "I should not have survived the explosion in Afghanistan. The fact that I am alive is a testament to the purpose I still have—to serve others."[3]

QUESTIONS FOR REFLECTION

Bouncing back from a setback doesn't necessarily mean returning to life as it was. To what degree are your hopes invested in going back to life as it was?

Is your faith deep enough to withstand a challenge as life altering as the one you just read? How can you stay strong in your faith to meet any of life's struggles?

CHAPTER 21

A MISSION OF MERCY

On a splendid April afternoon in 2008, two college women's softball teams—one from Oregon, one from Washington—squared off beneath the blue sky of the Cascade Mountains. Inside a chain link fence before a hundred fans, the two teams played a decisive game. The winner would advance to the NCAA division playoffs. The loser would hang up the gloves and go home.

The Western Oregon Wolves were a sturdy team that boasted several strong batters, but Sara Tucholsky was not one of them. She hit .153 and played in the game only because the first-string right fielder had muffed a play earlier in the day. Sara had never hit a home run, but on that Saturday, with two runners on base, she connected with a curveball and sent it sailing over the left-field fence.

In her excitement Sara missed first base. Her coach shouted for her to return and touch it. When she turned and started back, something popped in her knee, and down she went. She dragged herself back to the bag, pulled her knee to her chest in pain, and asked the first-base coach, "What do I do?"

The umpire wasn't sure. According to the rulebook, Sara would be out if any of her teammates assisted her. Sara knew if she tried to stand, she would collapse. Her team couldn't help her. Her leg couldn't support her. How could she cross home plate? The umpires huddled to talk.[1]

The rules did not say that the opposing team couldn't help.

Mallory Holtman came up with a solution.

She played first base for the opposing team, Central Washington University. She was a senior and wanted a victory. A loss would end her season. You'd think Mallory would be happy to see the home run nullified. She wasn't.

"Hey," she said to the umpires. "Can I help her around the bases?"

"Why would you want to do that?" one asked. Before she could answer, the ump shrugged and said, "Do it."

So Mallory did and teammate Liz Wallace helped too. The two walked toward the injured player. "We're going to pick you up and carry you around the bases." By this time tears streaked Sara's cheeks. "Thank you." Mallory and Liz put one hand under Sara's legs and the other hand under Sara's arms. The mission of mercy began. They paused long enough at second and third base to lower Sara's foot to touch the bases. By the time they headed home, the spectators had risen to their feet, Sara's teammates had gathered at home plate, and Sara was smiling like a homecoming queen.[2] This moment became one of the best examples of sportsmanship in the history of college sports.

QUESTIONS FOR REFLECTION

Have you experienced or witnessed an example of great sportsmanship? How did it change the game for you?

Have you seen this level of sportsmanship off the field, in everyday life?

Doug McKnight and family

Doug McKnight

CHAPTER 22

THE BURDEN OF DISCONTENT

T hink for just a moment about the things you own. Think about the house you have, the car you drive, the money you've saved. Think about the jewelry you've inherited and the stocks you've traded and the clothes you've purchased.

Your stuff isn't your stuff. Ask any coroner. Ask any embalmer. Ask any funeral-home director. No one takes anything with them.

When God thinks of you, he may see your compassion, your devotion, your tenderness, or quick mind, but he doesn't think of your things. And when you think of you, you shouldn't either. Define yourself by your stuff, and you'll feel good when you have a lot and bad when you don't.

Doug McKnight could say those words. At the age of thirty-two he was diagnosed with multiple sclerosis. Over the next sixteen years it would cost him his career, his mobility, and eventually his life. Because of MS, he couldn't feed himself or walk; he battled depression and fear. But through it all, Doug never lost his sense of gratitude. Evidence of this was seen in his prayer list. Friends in his congregation asked him to compile a list of requests so they could intercede for him. His response included eighteen blessings for which to be grateful and six concerns for which to be prayerful. His blessings outweighed his needs by three times. Doug McKnight had learned to be content.[1]

"Life is not defined by what you have, even when you have a lot" (Luke 12:15 MSG). Instead of being bitter and losing sight of what is important, Doug decided to approach life with gratitude and pray for the blessing of others.

QUESTIONS FOR REFLECTION

What is a source of discontent for you? How do you handle it?

How can you diminish its power over you?

Helen Roseveare

CHAPTER 23

I NEED HELP

Helen Roseveare was a missionary doctor who spent twenty years in the Congo at a clinic and orphanage. She lived through being brutally beaten, raped, and captured by Congo rebels. She used her captivity to encourage others who felt powerless to defend themselves against unimaginable acts of evil.

When Helen had been there almost four years, a mother died in labor, leaving behind a premature baby and a two-year-old girl. The facility had no incubator or electricity. Dr. Roseveare's first task was to keep the newborn warm. She sent a midwife to fetch a hot water bottle. The nurse returned with bad news: the bottle had burst when she filled it. Even worse, that was the last bottle. Dr. Roseveare instructed the midwife to sleep near the newborn. They would seek a solution the next day.

A solution was not easily found. The clinic was in the heart of the jungle. Help was many miles away. The life of the newborn was in jeopardy. The following noon the doctor mentioned the concern to the orphans. She told them of the frail baby and the sad sister. And they prayed.

A ten-year-old girl named Ruth decided on her own to take the problem to Jesus. "Please, God, send us a hot water bottle. It'll be no good tomorrow, God, as the baby'll be dead; so please send it this afternoon. And while you are about it, would you please send a dolly for the little two-year-old sister so she'll know you really love her?" The doctor was stunned. That prayer could only be answered by the arrival of a parcel from home. After nearly four years at the clinic, she'd never received a single package. Even if one came, who would send a hot water bottle to the equator?

Someone did. Later that afternoon a twenty-two-pound package was delivered to Helen's door. As she called the children, she felt tears in her eyes. Could it be? They pulled off the string and unwrapped the paper. In the box they found bandages, jerseys, raisins, sultanas, and a brand-new hot water bottle. And at the bottom of the box a doll for the little girl. The box had been shipped five months earlier.[1] It was packed by Helen's former Sunday school class, whose leader had heard and obeyed God's prompting to send a hot water bottle.

QUESTIONS FOR REFLECTION

Do you know someone like Dr. Helen Roseveare? Someone always willing to sacrifice everything for others?

Sending a hot water bottle and a doll probably seemed like an odd prompting by God. When is the last time you listened to God and obeyed an unusual prompting?

Freddy Vest

CHAPTER 24

THE POWER OF PRAYER

On July 28, 2008, championship roper Freddy Vest was preparing for his fourth ride at a Graham, Texas, calf roping when he fell off his horse. He was dead before he hit the ground. Cardiac arrest. A friend ran to his side, put his hand under Freddy's head, and began to pray. A veteran firefighter administered CPR and prayed as he pressed Freddy's chest. The friend asked everyone to pray, and the firefighter said he could hear people praying all around him. Soon the arena was a sanctuary of sorts, and Freddy was on the altar. He didn't respond. The firefighter team continued doing CPR on Freddy for forty-five minutes until the ambulance arrived. The men never gave up. They tried longer than most people would have deemed reasonable. They wanted to give Freddy every possible chance to survive.

Ambulance paramedics continued CPR, and while en route to Graham Hospital, they defibrillated Freddy's heart twice, and Freddy was airlifted to a Fort Worth hospital. His heart had to be restarted two more times during the flight.

Freddy's family and friends held a vigil while he was in surgery. Doctors were able to repair his heart but long-term expectations were unclear. Dr. Denzel D'Souza told the family that only about 9 percent of cardiac arrest patients survive. "And every minute that passes without defibrillation or restoration of blood flow," said Dr. D'Souza, "your mortality goes up 10 percent. For the brain you've got five, six minutes if you're lucky, ten at the outside—that's minutes—to get things going again. I actually was concerned that he was going to have brain damage."

Freddy, as it turns out, saw the prayers of the people. "I was with the Lord," he remembers. He describes a feeling of love, more love than anyone could imagine. He remembers a feeling of perfect peace, the kind of peace a child feels being held and rocked by his mother. Freddy remembers seeing the prayers. "God allowed me to see the prayers that came up for me. It started with one bolt of light. And then there were two bolts of light and three. Then there were ten. And then there were like hundreds, and then there were thousands of bolts of light. Each one of those bolts of light was a prayer that someone had sent up for me. And when there got to be so many bolts of light, it exploded into the brightest light . . . That's when God sent me back."[1]

The power of prayer was more than a gesture. Prayer saved Freddy's life.

QUESTIONS FOR REFLECTION

Describe a time you have been surprised by the power of prayer.

How has prayer affected your spiritual journey?

Nic Brown

Nic and Cassie Brown

CHAPTER 25

ROCK-STAR CAREGIVERS

Nic Brown was the first person in his county to be diagnosed with the coronavirus (COVID-19). He was thirty-eight years old at the time, a father of two daughters and a son, and husband to his wife, Cassie. As a resident of a rural county in Ohio, he has no idea how he contracted the disease. But he did.

Nic's medical history included bouts with asthma and heart arrhythmia. "When I got a headache and fever, and then a cough, I thought I had the flu," said Nic. Initially he went to a nearby urgent care. While being treated for pneumonia, he passed out. He was rushed to Cleveland Clinic Union Hospital in Dover, Ohio. There he tested positive for COVID-19. The disease attacked with a vengeance.

As his health declined, he was transferred to the medical intensive care unit and placed on full life support. His condition had so deteriorated that the hospital had end-of-life discussions with his wife. His medical team monitored his treatment by writing goals for each day on the glass door of his room. "They would encourage me. One day someone wrote, 'We will get you home.'"[1]

Little by little Nic's body began to combat the virus. The recovery was gradual, yet complete. Nic was eventually reunited with his children and his wife. The caretakers had kept their promise.[2] Too weak to write, Nic asked one of his nurses to transcribe a message to his caregivers:

> I watched you work hard to keep me and others alive, unable to thank you for the time that you poured into me—and although I will probably never get the chance to pour that same love and support into you, I want you to know that I think you all are rock stars.

"Part of why I [wrote] the note is because I don't know that I've ever seen such selfless people in my life. I really saw the love of God through them. They don't know me, but they cared for me like I was a member of their family. It's been life altering," says Nic.

QUESTIONS FOR REFLECTION

Have you or a loved one endured a dramatic COVID-19 experience? How has it changed your life?

Nic talks about pouring love and support into other people. How can you pour love and support into people within your community?

The *Spirit of Bermuda*. A bronze statue of Johnny Barnes.

CHAPTER 26

MR. HAPPY MAN

It's 6:00 A.M. in Hamilton, Bermuda. Ninety-two-year-old Johnny Barnes stands on the edge of a roundabout and waves at people as they drive past. He's been here since before 4:00 A.M. He'll be here until 10:00 A.M. He's not asking for money or begging for food. He's not protesting, complaining, picketing, or loitering.

He's making people happy.

He wears a straw hat and a salty beard. His eyes are bright, teeth white, and skin leathery and dark. The years have bent his back and slowed his step. But they haven't siphoned his joy. He waves with both hands extended in front of him. His wrists turn from side to side as if he were adjusting the volume on a soundboard.

He pulls back his right hand to retrieve a kiss and blow it in the direction of a taxi driver or commuter.

"I love you!" he shouts. "I'll love you forever!" "Hello, there, darlin'. I love you!"

And they love him! Bermudans call him Mr. Happy Man. They route their morning commute to see him. If Johnny's not standing in his spot, people call the radio station to check on him. If he happens to miss acknowledging some commuters, they often circle the round-about until he waves at them.

One morning a cranky woman determined not to make eye contact with him. She wanted to wallow in her bad mood. But she ended up looking his way. When he smiled, she smiled.

Another sour attitude bit the dust.

Johnny's philosophy is simple. "We human beings gotta learn how to love one another. One of the greatest joys that can come to an individual is when you're doing something and helping others."[1]

Johnny was born on June 23, 1923. His parents came to Bermuda from St. Kitts, a West Indian Island. He was an electrician and worked in the Bermuda Railways. In 1948 the railways closed, and Johnny became a bus driver. At sixty years old, on his way to work one day, he stopped at Crow Lane Circle and decided to wave at commuters and smile. He got an indescribable amount of joy and decided to quit his job so he could spread love to others for the rest of his life.

One day when Johnny took a sick day, the people of Bermuda were shaken and then wondered what they would do when Johnny Barnes was no more. The people of Bermuda created a charity called the *Spirit of Bermuda Trust*. People donated enough money to commission internationally famed sculptor Desmond Fountain, based in Bermuda, to create a $6^{1}/2$ foot bronze statue of Johnny.

On July 9, 2016, Johnny passed away at the age of ninety-three. In his last wish he said, "May my absence from the bench at the round-about and my statue, *The Spirit of Bermuda*, remind you to share love and kindness with each other . . . ."[2]

After Johnny's death *The Royal Gazette* spoke with Kenneth

Manders, president of the Bermuda Conference of the Seventh-day Adventists and Johnny's pastor for thirteen years at the Hamilton Seventh-day Adventist Church. "Brother Johnny Barnes represents what has become known as the spirit of Bermuda," Mr. Manders said. "His life, his love, his legacy has touched thousands of people in our community and those who have visited our country. His ministry has blessed people who were in need of prayer in the early morning. He was a Christian man and always tried to show the love of God and demonstrated that to all of mankind."

QUESTIONS FOR REFLECTION

How long has it been since you felt a level of contagious, infectious, unflappable, unstoppable happiness?

What can you do to live a happier life? What short-term and long-term changes should you make?

Tim Scott at the *USS Charleston*

Tim Scott speaking with workers

CHAPTER 27

SANDWICHES AND WISDOM

Tim was dealt a bad hand of cards. His parents divorced when he was seven years old. His mother, an African American nursing assistant, worked sixteen hours a day but still couldn't lift her family out of poverty. As a teenager, Tim served popcorn at the local Northwoods Mall movie theater while many of his friends were discovering video games and girls. During his break he would hurry across the street to a Chick-fil-A restaurant and get fries and water. John Moniz, a Citadel graduate and Air Force veteran, owned the facility. He noticed the repeat customer and asked him why he wasn't buying more food. Tim told him he couldn't afford it.

Moniz considered the plight of this teenage boy. He decided to encourage him. One evening he took a bag of sandwiches across the street. The two struck up a conversation that led to a friendship that led to a mentorship. Moniz learned that Tim was failing several classes at school, so Moniz shared with him life lessons about discipline and responsibility. He conveyed the biblical business principles he was using at his workplace. Most important, Moniz taught his young friend about Jesus.

Tim began eating up all the sandwiches and wisdom that Moniz had to give. The seventeen-year-old began to feel life coming together for him. Then tragedy struck. Moniz, at the age of thirty-seven, died of a pulmonary embolism. Tim was left standing at the graveside of his friend and at a crossroads. Much to his credit he chose to put the lessons Moniz had taught him to good use. He wrote a new purpose statement for his life. His mission? To have a positive effect on one billion people.

Pretty ambitious goal. Yet he appears to be well on his way to reaching it. Tim Scott was sworn in to the US Senate in 2013, the first African American senator from the South since Reconstruction.[1]

"Over the course of three or four years, John transformed my way of thinking, which changed my life. It was interesting because the lessons that John was teaching me were maybe simple lessons, but they were profound lessons," Tim said. "As I venture through life, business and politics, what I realize is that our greatest future is somehow connected to the folks who mentor us, who engage us in conversations that are in our enlightened best interest, but the manifestation of which might not occur for decades. I'd like to encourage all mentors to not only be a mentor but to know the difference they are making may not actually manifest itself for a decade or two. In my life, not only did John Moniz transform my thinking, but he changed my life."

Tim goes on to say, "Many of the lessons he taught me never manifested themselves until after he sadly passed away. He will never know how thankful I am that he never gave up on me, that he was wise enough to know that growth takes time, especially for a teenager."[2]

It all started with a sandwich and a fellow who was willing to walk across the street and offer some encouragement. Maybe we could do something similar?

QUESTIONS FOR REFLECTION

Has there been someone in your life who saw your possibilities, your promise? How did he or she demonstrate confidence in you?

Have you been an encourager to someone? Explain.

Dr. Eben Alexander

CHAPTER 28

THE POWER POSTURE

R ather than fretting about the future of your family, pray for them. Rather than assuming you can do nothing to help others, assume the posture of prayer.

At 4:30 A.M. on November 10, 2008, Eben Alexander's brain began to fail him. Pain shot through his body. He dismissed it as a virus he'd been battling for several days. Within a couple of hours he knew it was more. He was in agony and virtually paralyzed. By 9:30 A.M. his body was stiff and spasmic. His eyes rolled back in his head, and he slipped into a coma.

The surprising and difficult diagnosis was a rare form of E. coli bacterial meningitis: meningoencephalitis. No one could explain its origin. No one dared to hope for survival. Fewer than one in ten million adults contract it annually. His odds of survival were estimated at 2 percent.

Ironically the man with the failing brain was a brain surgeon. Dr. Alexander's résumé impresses even the most educated scholar. Duke University School of Medicine. Residency at Massachusetts

General Hospital and Harvard. A fellowship in cerebrovascular neuro-surgery. Fifteen years on the faculty of Harvard Medical School. Countless brain surgeries. Author of more than 150 chapters and articles for medical publications. Presentations at more than two hundred medical conferences worldwide.

After Dr. Alexander had been in a coma for a week, the doctors began to prepare his family for the worst news.

Irony number two: Dr. Alexander was not a spiritual man. He would be the first to tell you he was a realist. He used the tools of modern medicine to heal people. No one was more surprised than he at what he saw during the coma. "There was a whooshing sound, and in a flash I went through the opening and found myself in a completely new world." In this place "shimmering beings arced across the sky." He heard "a sound, huge and booming like a glorious chant." He describes an "explosion of light, color, love, and beauty that blew through [him] like a crashing wave. . . . There seemed to be no dis-tance at all between God and myself."

What was happening? Prayer was happening. The doctor may not have been a spiritual man, but his friends and family were. In Lynchburg General Hospital they began to gather. They knew to pray. Individually and as a community. As the days passed, they wondered if their prayers mattered. On Thursday, three days into the coma, the pastor of their church was called, and a final wave of urgent prayers began, and the prayers began to break through.

Dr. Alexander wrote, "I moved down through great walls of clouds. There was murmuring all around me, but I couldn't understand the words. Then I realized that countless beings were surrounding me, kneeling in arcs that spread into the distance. Looking back on it now, I realize what these half-seen, half-sensed hierarchies of beings, stretching out into the dark above and below, were doing. They were praying for me."[1]

On Sunday morning he awoke from his coma. Prayers brought the doctor back to earth.

QUESTIONS FOR REFLECTION

Intercessory prayer is the act of praying on another's behalf. Is this type of prayer a part of your daily life? Why or why not?

Think of a time you prayed for someone and the prayer was answered the way you hoped.

Lieutenant Colonel Brian Reed with
1st Stryker Brigade Combat Team

CHAPTER 29

BREAKING BREAD

Lieutenant Colonel Brian Reed served in a military unit in Baghdad, Iraq, in the fall of 2003. He and his unit went on regular street patrols to protect neighborhoods and build peace. It was often a thankless, fruitless assignment. Citizens seemed more interested in receiving a handout than a hand up. Brian said his unit battled low morale daily.

An exception came in the form of a church service his men stumbled upon. The soldiers got out of their military vehicles, intrigued by the sight of a wrought iron nativity: three wise men from the East advertising to all who passed by that this was a Christian gathering in a Christian church.

Brian and his men, armed and armored to the teeth, entered the facility. It was filled with Arabic-speaking Coptic Christians singing and praising God with a worship team and PowerPoint slides. The Americans did not understand a word, but they recognized the image on the screen, a depiction of Jesus. The language was foreign, but the observances were not: fellowship, prayer, the teaching, and the breaking of bread.

When they saw the American soldiers, the Coptic Christians invited them to partake in the Lord's Supper with them. The soldiers removed their helmets and received the sacraments. They then joined the Iraqis on a processional as they made their way out of the sanctuary into a courtyard that ended at the foot of a large wooden cross.

Afterward they smiled, laughed, shook hands, and prayed again. It was peace in the Middle East.

Brian wrote, "Jesus was there. He showed up in the very place some of us were ready for our air force brethren to blow off the face of the earth. God spoke to me that evening. . . . Celebrating the Lord's Supper and remembering Jesus' sacrifice for our sins was the most important bridge builder and wall destroyer we could have experienced."[1]

They were "opposite yous" brought together by the cross of Christ. This is happiness.

QUESTIONS FOR REFLECTION

Have you experienced a situation where opposites were brought together by the cross of Christ?

In your history of breaking bread, has there been an instance when an unlikely friendship was formed? Do you think that kinship would be as strong if you hadn't decided to welcome openness with a meal?

Jake Olson at USC football game

Coach Pete Carroll

CHAPTER 30

MAKE SOMEONE HAPPY

One of the biggest moments in the history of the University of Southern California football does not include a trophy hoist or a touchdown dash. In my opinion the event that deserves a spot in the Hall of Fame includes no game-winning pass or Gatorade-drenched coach. If given the chance to stand on the sidelines and watch one moment of the storied program that began in 1888, I would select 2017, USC versus Western Michigan. With three minutes and thirteen seconds to go in the fourth quarter, USC intercepted a pass for a touchdown and took a solid 48–31 lead. A few of the 61,125 fans began walking toward the Los Angeles Memorial Coliseum exits. The rest of the game, it appeared, was a formality.

But then head coach Clay Helton shouted for Jake Olson, a redshirt sophomore, to take the field to deep snap the football for the extra point.

What makes the moment historic and unforgettable is not that a player was called off the bench. The unique stand-up-and-watch-this-ness of the play was that the player was blind. That's right. Jake Olson trotted onto a field that was, to him, cast in midnight black. He could not see the smiling faces of the other Trojans in the huddle. He was unable to see the row of teammates on the sideline, all standing, all watching. He had no vision of the coaches who, with blurry eyes and tight throats, knew they were watching a dream come true.

Jake Olson's journey toward this game began at the age of ten months when he lost his left eye to retinal cancer. The cancer returned when he was twelve years old. Doctors determined that the only way to contain the cancer was to remove the right eye also.

Pete Carroll was the USC head coach at the time. A mutual friend of the Olson family told him about a boy who was a lifelong Trojan fan and about to lose his sight. Carroll set out to fill Jake's head with USC football memories: he arranged for Jake to meet players, participate in pre- and post-practice huddles, and hold the traditional band leader's sword and direct the band after a game. Jake even traveled to Notre Dame with the team.

Then came the darkness.

When he was healthy enough to attend a team practice after the surgery, he was welcomed as if he'd won the Heisman.

When Carroll took a job with the Seattle Seahawks, he invited Olson to join his team on the sidelines for a game. That's when the center for the team asked Olson if he'd ever deep snapped a football. Blindness could keep Olson from throwing, tackling, blocking, and catching, but launching the ball between his legs to a holder eight yards away? Olson learned to do it. He made it his dream to play in at least one USC game.

To make it happen the coaches of the two teams had to talk. The Western Michigan squad agreed not to crush Olson with a rushing linebacker. The USC coaching staff agreed to use Olson only after the game was out of reach for one of the two teams. The school cleared the decision with the Pac-12 conference. Jake suited up and awaited his opportunity.

For most of the game Olson's moment was in doubt. The score was 14–14 at half, 21–21 after three quarters. With six minutes to go in the game, the teams were knotted at 28–28. But then USC caught fire, scored three times, and put the game away.

Coach Helton called time-out. Olson took a couple of practice snaps. While he warmed up, Helton signaled to the Western Michigan coach, who signaled to his team. Every player on both sides of the field perked up. The official, also in on the drama, spotted the ball, placed a hand on Olson's back, stepped out of the way, and whistled for the play to begin.

At that moment there were no competitors, no opposing sides, no winners and losers. There was only one player overcoming a massive handicap, and everyone rooted for him.

In the history of college football, the game was but one of thousands. The moment, however, was one in a million. On cue Olson spiraled a perfect snap. The ball was placed, the kick was good, and Jake was mobbed by his teammates.

It was, perhaps, the greatest extra point in the history of the Trojans.[1]

Jake Olson was the first blind long snapper in college football. "Jake's a huge story and he's one for all of us about courage and character and grit and vision and special qualities that few people would be able to hold on to," said Coach Carroll.[2]

Happiness has a way of cascading forth when humanity is unselfish enough to help others have their moment.

QUESTIONS FOR REFLECTION

Do you feel that happiness is luck, or is it a practiced mind-set? Why?

How can you bring more happiness to others? How are your own wants getting in the way of helping someone else be happy?

Dr. Maxwell Maltz

CHAPTER 31

SELFLESS LOVE

Dr. Maxwell Maltz, a Christian and prominent plastic surgeon, tells a remarkable story of unconditional love. A man had been injured in a fire while attempting to save his parents from a burning house. He couldn't get to them. They perished. His face was burned and disfigured. He mistakenly interpreted his pain as God's punishment. The man wouldn't let anyone see him—not even his wife.

She went to Dr. Maltz, a plastic surgeon, for help. He told the woman not to worry. "I can restore his face."

The wife was unenthused. Her husband had repeatedly refused any help. She knew he would again.

Then why her visit? "I want you to disfigure my face so I can be like him! If I can share in his pain, then maybe he will let me back into his life."

Dr. Maltz was shocked. He denied her request but was so moved by this woman's love that he went to speak with her husband. Knocking on the man's bedroom door, he called loudly, "I'm a plastic surgeon, and I want you to know that I can restore your face."

No response.

"Please come out."

Again there was no answer.

Still speaking through the door, Dr. Maltz told the man of his wife's proposal. "She wants me to disfigure her face, to make her face like yours in the hope that you will let her back into your life. That's how much she loves you."

There was a brief moment of silence, and then ever so slowly the doorknob began to turn.[1] The wife's choice echoes that of Jesus. Our Savior took on our face, our disfigurement. He became like us. Just look at the places he was willing to go. The places he went to reach us show how far he will go to touch us. He loves to be with the ones he loves.

QUESTIONS FOR REFLECTION

What do you think finally got through to the man? What force drove him to change his mind?

Have you ever experienced human love as great as that of the wife in the story? Explain.

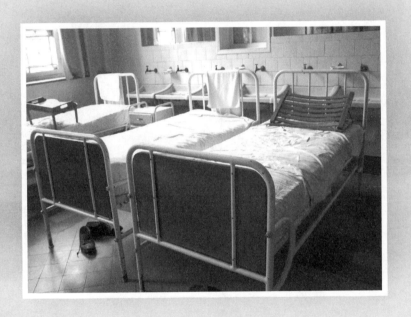

CHAPTER 32

A BRAVE VOLUNTEER

On February 15, 1921, in New York City at the Kane Summit Hospital, a doctor is performing an appendectomy.

In many ways the events leading to the surgery are uneventful. The patient has complained of severe abdominal pain. The diagnosis is clear: an inflamed appendix. Dr. Evan O'Neill Kane is performing the surgery. In his distinguished thirty-seven-year medical career, he has performed nearly four thousand appendectomies, so this surgery will be uneventful in all ways except two.

The first novelty of this operation? The use of local anesthesia in major surgery. Dr. Kane is a crusader against the hazards of general anesthesia. He contends that a local application is far safer. Many of his colleagues agree with him in principle, but in order for them to agree in practice, they will have to see the theory applied.

Dr. Kane searches for a volunteer, a patient who is willing to undergo surgery while under local anesthesia. A volunteer is not easily found. Many are squeamish at the thought of being awake during their own surgery. Others are fearful that the anesthesia might wear off too soon.

Eventually, however, Dr. Kane finds a candidate. On Tuesday morning, February 15, the historic operation occurs.

The patient is prepped and wheeled into the operating room. A local anesthetic is applied. As he has done thousands of times, Dr. Kane dissects the superficial tissues and locates the appendix. He skillfully excises it and concludes the surgery. During the procedure the patient complains of only minor discomfort.

The volunteer is taken into post op and then placed in a hospital ward. He recovers quickly and is dismissed two days later.

Dr. Kane had proved his theory. Thanks to the willingness of a brave volunteer, Kane demonstrated that local anesthesia was a viable, and even preferable, alternative.

But I said there were two facts that made the surgery unique. I've told you the first: the use of local anesthesia. The second is the patient. The courageous candidate for surgery by Dr. Kane was Dr. Kane.

To prove his point, Dr. Kane operated on himself![1]

A wise move. The doctor became a patient in order to convince the patients to trust the doctor.

I've shared this story with several health professionals. They all gave me the same response: furrowed brow, suspicious grin, and the dubious words "That's hard to believe."

Perhaps it is. But the story of the doctor who became his own patient is mild compared to the story of the God who became human. But Jesus did. So that you and I would believe that the Healer knows our hurts, he voluntarily became one of us. He placed himself in our position. He suffered our pains and felt our fears.

QUESTIONS FOR REFLECTION

Is there a doctor or nurse you admire? Has he or she gone out of the way to make your health a priority?

When is the last time you properly thanked the health professionals in your life? How can you make them feel appreciated and recognized?

The Miracles choir, taken March 2023 at the Baddour Center Chapel. There are 18 choir members.

CHAPTER 33

MIRACLES

The Miracles are a nationally recognized choir out of Senatobia, Mississippi, made up of twenty people with special needs and the stouthearted. Just see if you can listen to them and still feel sorry for yourself.

Their ministry is to glorify God, demonstrate the abilities of persons with intellectual disabilities, and tell the story of the Baddour Center. Amy Twilley, the Miracles' director, believes that the choir helps members in many ways. "Musically, the members learn to sing musically, learn to sing in harmony, and learn to be expressive. Spiritually, the residents introduce the songs. The residents share devotions and pray at rehearsals by using Scripture memory songs as vocal warm-ups. As team players, the residents work together to learn new songs, to sound like one voice (no popcorn singers), and have duties that require them to move and set up equipment. Confidence-wise, all members introduce themselves during the performance, introduce the songs, and visit with the audience. The experience provides the opportunity not only to see new areas of the country but to meet new people while representing Baddour—something they take great pride in."

The Miracles program was established in 1979 by the center's chaplain at the time, Reverend Robbie Hammons. The program was initially inspired by a resident who was very gifted at playing the piano. Then in the 1980s the number grew to thirty-five residents with all residents living at the Baddour Center. Eventually the choir transitioned into an auditioned choir with an established twenty-one residents.

The choir travels across the United States to express their faith through music, to bridge attitudinal barriers that may exist toward adults with intellectual disabilities, and to share God's Good News. Prior to the 2020 pandemic, during peak years their annual travels included an average of seven thousand miles, forty-four performances, and approximately seven thousand people in churches and other venues.

The Miracles are supported by several churches of many denominations that donate regularly and/or schedule the choir to perform at their church.

QUESTIONS FOR REFLECTION

Do you have a loved one with special needs? If so, how have opportunities similar to the Miracles helped him or her excel and build confidence?

Does your community or neighborhood support special needs groups? How can you become more involved and help them spread God's message?

Outside of Humaita Prison

Inside Humaita Prison

CHAPTER 34

HANDCUFFED BY LOVE

Near the city of São José dos Campos, Brazil, is a remarkable facility. Several decades ago the Brazilian government turned the Humaita Prison over to two Christian volunteers who later became part of Prison Fellowship Brazil. The institution is run on Christian principles. With the exception of two full-time staff members, all the work is done by inmates. Families outside the prison adopt a prisoner to work with during and after the inmate's term.

Inside, the walls are covered with inspirational quotes. "It is not enough to stop doing evil; it is necessary to do good." "All honest work is blessed by God."

The prison is divided into three security levels: closed, for maximum security; a semiopen stage, in which the men learn a trade; and open, in which they live at home but work full-time and report to the prison every day.

When an inmate enters the prison at the closed stage, his handcuffs are removed by a volunteer who says, "In this prison your heart is handcuffed by love, and you are watched over by Christ."

The prison aims to help inmates reconcile with the people they hurt and find peace for themselves. This salvation is possible because of two volunteers who believed in the power of redemption.

Charles Colson, the founder of Prison Fellowship, visited the prison and made this report:

> When I visited Humaita, I found the inmates smiling—particularly the murderer who held the keys, opened the gates, and let me in. Wherever I walked I saw men at peace. I saw clean living areas, people working industriously. The walls were decorated with biblical sayings from Psalms and Proverbs. . . . My guide escorted me to the notorious prison cell once used for torture. Today, he told me, that block houses only a single inmate. As we reached the end of a long concrete corridor and he put the key in the lock, he paused and asked, "Are you sure you want to go in?"
>
> "Of course," I replied impatiently, "I've been in isolation cells all over the world." Slowly he swung open the massive door, and I saw the prisoner in that punishment cell: a crucifix, beautifully carved by the Humaita inmates—the prisoner Jesus, hanging on a cross.
>
> "He's doing time for the rest of us," my guide said softly.[1]

QUESTIONS FOR REFLECTION

Accountability fosters better relationships, improves overall happiness, and creates community. How has accountability affected your life? How have you been empowered by accountability?

Why do you think restorative justice is important?

Stephanie Decker visiting the White House
and meeting President Barack Obama

CHAPTER 35

UNFAILING LOVE

The world saw a glimpse of unfailing love on March 2, 2012. During an unusually harsh season of tornadoes that crashed and trenched the American Midwest, a young mother demonstrated her unfailing love for her two children. As her house in Henryville, Indiana, was sliced and shredded by relentless winds, Stephanie Decker shielded eight-year-old Dominic and five-year-old Reese with her body. She wrapped her children in a blanket, lay down on top of them, and held on with all her might.

"I grabbed the kids, and I wasn't letting go," said the Indiana mom. "If they were going to fly, I was going to fly with them." She watched the foundation separate from the house and lift up. The F4 tornado with 175-mile-an-hour winds tore through their home.

"I could see it in slow motion," she says. "I was covered in bricks and stones. I could let go of them, move the stuff off me, and get away from that beam. I chose to let the beam fall instead of letting go of my kids. The feeling was, I'd rather get my arms ripped off instead of letting go of my kids."

Her legs were crushed and trapped under a beam as another tornado, an F2, headed their way to rip a pillar off their home.

"The pillar was coming straight for my daughter's head," she says. "Now that I only have upper-body movement I can't cover them. So I'm twisting back and forth, taking the brunt of the flying debris. I twisted my body and broke eight ribs and punctured my lung."[1]

Her determination paid off. The children and their mom survived. But in the violent storm, Stephanie lost both of her legs.

What would drive a mother to do such a thing? Love.

Stephanie shared her unfailing love with others by starting the Stephanie Decker Foundation a year after the tornado. The foundation supports children who have lost limbs by providing equal access to leading-edge prosthetics regardless of their financial situation. Stephanie also travels across the country as a motivational speaker. "I love the impossible," she says. "That's my forte."

QUESTIONS FOR REFLECTION

When was the last time you sacrificed everything for love? What was the outcome?

Instead of allowing the tragic events to negatively alter her life, Stephanie has chosen to share her unfailing love with others. Have you ever turned a bad situation into one that shares unfailing love with others? What did you do? How has that situation changed the way you live your life?

Max's
Personal
Stories

CHAPTER 36

THIS CHILD IS MINE

Perhaps you can relate to this tender childhood memory. My parents and grandparents conspired for me to spend a week under the care of my grandmother and grandfather. I may have been ten years old, if that. I was just a lad. The plan was simple: Mom and Dad would drive me to the bus station, buy me a ticket, and see me off on the three-hour trek. My grandparents would drive to the bus station closest to their house, await my arrival, and take me to their home. My job, as recited multiple times by my mother, was to plant myself in the seat and not get off at any of the stops along the way. If I did get off, it was to be only for reasons of biological necessity. "Do your business, talk to no one, and get back on board." If Mom said it once, she said it a dozen times.

She had reason to be worried, of course. The road can be a treacherous place. Kids get lost. Kids get snatched. Kids get rebellious. Despite the danger, my parents took me to the bus station.

As I was about to step onto the bus, my dad did a reassuring thing. He took a small amount of cash, paired it with a prewritten note, and stuck both in my shirt pocket. "Buy yourself some candy." He gave me a hug. Mom gave me a kiss. Off I went.

As per my instructions I stayed put and watched the West Texas cotton fields blur past. We stopped at thriving towns like Seminole, Slaton, and Idalou, but I didn't exit. Only when I spotted my grandma did I climb down from the bus. The trip went off without a hitch.

Indeed, the only reason it deserves to be mentioned is because of the note Dad stuck in my shirt pocket. Just a few miles into the trip I retrieved the money and the slip of paper. "This boy belongs to Jack and Thelma Lucado," it read. The note contained our home address and phone number. In the unlikely event that I was separated from the bus, this message, he hoped, would reconnect me to my family.

It brings me great joy to say this: God did the same with you. Look into the shirt pocket of your spirit, and you will see it. He laid public claim to you: "This child is mine." You and I need the protection. The road can be a treacherous place. His kids get lost. His sons and daughters grow rebellious. The Evil One can lure us. God wants Satan and Satan's minions to know, "This one belongs to me. Keep your hands off."

QUESTIONS FOR REFLECTION

If you had experienced such a trip as a child, whose names would have been written on your piece of paper? Who gave you a secure sense of belonging? How did this feeling of belonging affect you as you were growing up?

If you did not grow up with a strong sense of belonging, how did that affect you? Why do you think it's important to have a secure sense of belonging to your family, friends, and community?

CHAPTER 37

THE CASE OF THE SLEEPING GRANDPA

We weren't yet teenagers. Close, but not quite. Barely in middle school. Unwhiskered. Pimpled. A bit awkward and probably in need of some discipline. Three of us boys comprised the entirety of a Bible class at church. Our teacher devised a plan that, I suppose, was intended to develop our leadership skills.

We paid Sunday evening visits to elderly folks who were unable to attend morning church services. Shut-ins, we called them. Health issues and aging bodies had left these people shut in and unable to get out.

Most of our visits took place in a small and rather unfavorably fragrant convalescent home on the outskirts of our small town. The patients seemed happy to see the church deacon and his young disciples. Our liturgy was a simple one. We stood in a horseshoe around the foot of each bed. The teacher would share a brief lesson. One of us would read a scripture. Another would say a prayer.

If requested, we sang a hymn. And we would serve Communion. We traveled with a small box of wafers, grape juice, and cups.

A good way for young men to spend a Sunday evening. Right?

But then came the case of the sleeping grandpa. I do not recall why the teacher wasn't with us. I do recall that we were flying solo. Someone deposited us at the front door of the convalescent home. We divided up the responsibilities. One to say the prayer. One to read a scripture, and yours truly was left with the Communion kit.

We were the Protestant version of altar boys.

All went well until we encountered the slumbering man. He was in his bed, flat on his back with mouth open. The TV volume was loud, but his snoring was louder. "Sir," we said. No response. One of us touched his shoulder. Another gave him a shake. He just snorted.

We didn't think to ask a nurse for help. Turning and leaving was unacceptable. How dare we shirk our task?

So as the television roared and the old man snored, we did our duty. Prayer. Scripture, and, well, it was my turn. My friends looked at me. I looked at the man. His face was drawn, hair was gray, and mouth still wide open.

I did the only thing I knew to do. I placed a wafer on his tongue and washed it down with a cup of grape juice. We turned and scurried out of the room. He slept through the whole thing.

We've been known to do the same. We grow drowsy in our spirituality. Vibrancy is replaced by lethargy. Enthusiasm fades, and, well, we doze off. I'm not talking about hard-hearted rebels or cynics who reject God. I'm talking about the good-hearted saints who experience a dry heart, a waning love—who feel a disconnect in their relationship with God.

QUESTIONS FOR REFLECTION

Can you relate to growing drowsy in your spirituality? A disconnection from God?

Has anyone helped you through such a time, either knowingly or unknowingly? Describe his or her help.

During spiritually dry times, ask the Holy Spirit to breathe life into every dry bone in your body, and trust that the Spirit can give you new life.

CHAPTER 38

POCKETS FULL OF ROCKS

God does not stand on a ladder and tell us to climb it and find him. He lowers a ladder in the wilderness of our lives and finds us. He does not offer to use us if we behave. He pledges to use us, knowing all the while we will misbehave. Grace is not a gift for those who avoid the shadows of Shechem. Grace exists because none of us succeed in doing so.

God loving. God stooping. God offering. God caring and God carrying.

Do you know this grace?

Grace does for us what I did for my grandson. Denalyn and I were enjoying an afternoon chat when, from outside our back door, I heard these words: "Help! It's an emergency!"

I knew the voice because I know the girl. Rosie, our granddaughter. She was one month shy of six years, redheaded, blue-eyed, and in that moment sounding as if something was urgent.

Rosie and her three-year-old brother, Max Wesley, were engaged in their favorite pastime—rock collecting. No need to spend money on toys for this duo. Just turn them loose in the open field behind our house so they can search for glittering, sparkly stones.

As we hurried out the back door, Jenna asked Rosie, "What happened?"

"Max can't stand up!"

I assumed the worst. Rattlesnake bite. A tumble into the ravine.

"Why can't he stand up?"

"He loaded rocks in his pockets. His pants fell down to his ankles. He's stuck and can't stand up."

We stopped, looked at each other, and smiled.

"Looks like a sermon illustration in the making," Denalyn told me.

She was right. It was an illustration deluxe. Little Max could not stand up. He was plopped on the path. His knees were drawn to his chest. His jeans were down to his ankles. The only thing separating his rear from the asphalt was Spiderman underwear.

"Can you get up?" I asked.

His voice was small and forlorn. "No."

"Can you try?"

When he did, the problem was all too clear. Each pocket was laden with rocks. Side pockets, rear pockets, all four pockets made heavy with stones.

"Do you need help?" I asked.

He said, "Yes." He let me help him remove the unnecessary loads one by one, rock by rock, weight by weight. Next thing you know he hitched up his jeans and began to play again.

QUESTIONS FOR REFLECTION

What keeps you from rising up? What entangles your feet? What prevents you from moving forward? What load pilfers your peace?

Would you follow Max's example?

CHAPTER 39

GOD'S NEVER-ENDING GRACE

A few years ago our family went on vacation to the beach. Rosie, grandchild number one, was three-and-a-half years old and had never seen the ocean. We all wondered how she would respond to the sight. When she saw the waves and heard the roar of the water, she watched and listened and then finally asked, "When does it turn off?"

It doesn't, sweetie.

We ask the same about God's grace. Surely it will dry up and stop flowing, right? Wrong. Surely we will exhaust his goodness, won't we? Never. We will at some point write one too many checks on his mercy and love, correct? Incorrect.

> He doesn't treat us as our sins deserve,
>> nor pay us back in full for our wrongs.
> As high as heaven is over the earth,
>> so strong is his love to those who fear him.
> And as far as sunrise is from sunset,
>> he has separated us from our sins.

As parents feel for their children,
GOD feels for those who fear him.

(Ps. 103:10–13 MSG)

"Can anything make me stop loving you?" God asks. "Watch me speak your language, sleep on your earth, and feel your hurts. Behold the maker of sight and sound as he sneezes, coughs, and blows his nose. You wonder if I understand how you feel? Look into the dancing eyes of the kid in Nazareth; that's God walking to school. Ponder the toddler at Mary's table; that's God spilling his milk.

"You wonder how long my love will last? Find your answer on a splintered cross, on a craggy hill. That's me you see up there, your Maker, your God, nail-stabbed and bleeding. Covered in spit and sin-soaked. That's your sin I'm feeling. That's your death I'm dying. That's your resurrection I'm living. That's how much I love you."

"Can anything come between you and me?" asks the firstborn Son.

Hear the answer, and stake your future on the triumphant words of Paul: "I am sure that neither death, nor life, nor angels, nor ruling spirits, nothing now, nothing in the future, no powers, nothing above us, nothing below us, nor anything else in the whole world will ever be able to separate us from the love of God that is in Christ Jesus our Lord" (Rom. 8:38–39 NCV).

QUESTIONS FOR REFLECTION

If you truly believed that God's grace was never-ending like the oceans' tides, how would it affect your life? How would it change the way you interact with others?

How might it alter the way you view yourself?

CHAPTER 40

A FAMILY TALE

My wife's family is a repository of great stories. When I am with them, I keep a notebook handy because I know someone will share something worth retelling. Among my favorites is the account of a trip from Tulsa to Los Angeles. The primary characters in the episode are Uncle Ellis and his son-in-law Pat. Back in the early '90s, as the story goes, they drove Pat's son to Los Angeles so the boy could take a shot at an acting career.

Uncle Ellis was in his sixties at the time and pretty set in his ways. He didn't take to being away from home. The idea was to travel nonstop from Tulsa to L.A., spend one night in the big city, and head back.

Turned out, even one night was too many. Ellis saw the hustle of Los Angeles and changed his mind. He and Pat dropped the young man at his destination and turned the truck around with every intent of driving nonstop to Oklahoma. But as the sun began to set, their eyelids grew heavy. They made it as far as Arizona before they decided to spend the night.

About 5:00 P.M. they found a hotel with an adjacent diner. They checked into a room with two beds. Ellis called his wife and informed her of their plans. The two men then went to the restaurant. They found an unoccupied booth and ordered breakfast for supper. By 6:30 they had eaten, cleaned up, gone to bed, and fallen fast asleep.

Thirty minutes later Pat rolled over and noticed the time on the digital clock said 7:00. He mistakenly assumed it was 7:00 A.M., not 7:00 P.M., and that it was time to get out of bed and hit the road. He woke up his father-in-law and told him it was time to leave. Ellis grumbled something about the short night. Still, he climbed out of bed.

They checked out of the hotel and decided it would be prudent to eat breakfast before getting on the highway. (After all, they thought it was 7:00 A.M.) They entered the same restaurant, sat at the same booth, were served by the same attendant, and ordered the same breakfast. It didn't occur to them to ask why she was still on duty. It didn't occur to her to ask why the same two men were ordering the same meal she had served them an hour earlier.

By now it was 8:00 P.M., though Ellis and Pat thought it was 8:00 A.M. As they drove toward Tulsa, one told the other, "The sky seems to be getting darker, not brighter." By 9:00 P.M. (or 9:00 A.M. in their imaginations) the sky was black, and the stars were out, and Ellis and Pat were spooked. They pulled over to the side of the road. Ellis called his wife and told her to get her stuff ready because the world was about to end and the Battle of Armageddon was about to begin.

"Honey," she replied, "you called just three hours ago. What are you doing back out on the road?" Only then did Ellis realize they'd misinterpreted the time.

They aren't the first to make such a mistake. This journey toward home can bewilder the best of us. Truth be told, we've all lost track of time. We've lost our bearings. We've lost our perspective. At one time or another we've all needed help. We need to be reminded where we are and where we're headed. For Ellis and Pat, it was a voice from home.

For us, it's the name of Jesus, sweetest name ever spoken.

I know, I know. The name *Jesus* has been derided and mocked, turned into a curse word and a scapegoat for everything from a hammered thumb to medieval Crusades. Peeling back all the layers from the name is no easy task. But it is one worth the effort.

To see me is to see God, Jesus said. His voice, God's voice. His tears, God's tears. Want to know what matters to God? Find out what matters to Jesus. Want to know what in the world God is doing? Ponder the words of Jesus. Need to know where history is headed? He wrote the time line.

It could be that your experience with the name of Jesus has been less than positive. Did someone ram some frosty ideas about right and wrong down your throat and tell you they started with Jesus? Did a circle of high and mighty folks keep you out because you weren't good enough? Or maybe no one needs to tell you anything. You've fumbled enough footballs in life to know that no one like Jesus would have a spot for someone like you.

Reconsider, won't you?

What if he really is who he claims to be? The image of the invisible God. And what if he can do what he claimed to do? Lead wayward travelers like you and me onto the right road. Maybe it's time to pull over to the side of the road and make a call.

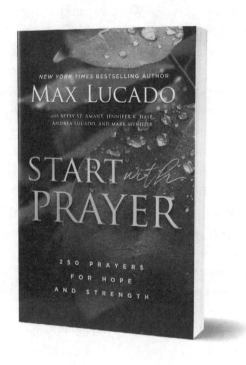

Start with Prayer is a special collection of 250 topically arranged prayers, designed to help you find the strength and hope you need before you try to solve the problem on your own. It is the perfect go-to when you want to pray but lack the words to do so.

WWW.MAXLUCADO.COM

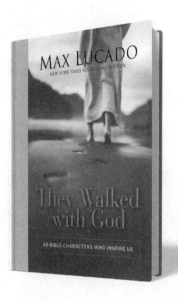

They Walked with God takes a closer look at forty of the most inspirational characters in the Bible and shares a powerful message: if God can find a place for each character in the Bible, he's carved out a spot for you too.

WWW.MAXLUCADO.COM

NOTES

A STORY OF SALVATION

1. Captain Eddie Rickenbacker, "Guideposts Classics: Eddie Rickenbacker on Helping Others," https://guideposts.org/prayer/power-of-prayer/guideposts -classics-eddie-rickenbacker-on-helping-others/.
2. Billy A. Rea, "Eddie Rickenbacker—and Six Other People Crash in the Pacific," History Net, June 12, 2006, https://www.historynet.com/eddie- rickenbacker-and-six-other-people-survive-a-b-17-crash-and-three-weeks-lost -in-the-pacific-ocean.

OPEN MIND, OPEN HEART

1. David Aikman, *Great Souls: Six Who Changed the Century* (Nashville: Word Publishing, 1998), 341–42.
2. Aikman, *Great Souls,* 338–44.

HUMBLE HEART

1. Dan McCarney, "Courage to Quit," *San Antonio Express News,* 13 July 2000, sec. 4C.
2. Nick Zaccardi, "Esther Kim, Who Gave Her Olympic Spot to Best Friend, Dies at 40," NBC Sports, December 13, 2019, https://olympics.nbcsports .com/2019/12/13/esther-kim-dies/.

THE ANGEL OF SING SING

1. Tim Kimmel, quoted in Stu Weber, *Tender Warrior* (Sisters, Ore.: Multnomah Books, 1993), excerpted as "Changed Lives" in *A 4th Course of Chicken Soup for the Soul* (Deerfield, Fla.: Health Communications, 1997), 60–61.

SOMEONE WORTH SAVING

1. Barbara Bressi-Donahue, "Friends of the Ring," *Reader's Digest*, June 1999, 154.
2. Bressi-Donahue, "Friends of the Ring," 153–60.

ANGELS AMONG US

1. This story initially appeared in Max Lucado, *The Gift for All People: Thoughts on God's Great Grace (Colorado Springs, CO: Multnomah, 2016)*. Thanks to Multnomah Publishing for allowing us to use it in *Traveling Light* and *Begin Again*.

EAGLES OVER WOLVES

1. Rick Reilly, "Eagles over Wolves in a Rout," ESPN, February 14, 2011, https://www.espn.com/espn/news/story?id=6120346.

RECYCLED HOPE

1. Sixty Minutes Staff, "Price of Success: Will the Recycled Orchestra Last?" CBSNews.com, November 17, 2013, www.cbsnews.com/news/price-of-success-will-the-recycled-orchestra-last/.

UNPACK YOUR BAGS

1. From a conversation with Jimmy Wayne and used by permission. For a full account see Jimmy Wayne with Ken Abraham, *Walk to Beautiful: The Power of Love and a Homeless Kid Who Found the Way* (Nashville: W Publishing, 2014).

COMFORTED BY A STRANGER

1. From a conversation with Tammy Trent and used by permission.

GRIEF AND GRATEFULNESS

1. My late friend Tim Hansel said something similar in his book *You Gotta Keep Dancin'* (Colorado Springs: Victor Books, 1985), 107.
2. Rachel Quigley, "'I Have a Tomorrow Because of Taylor': the Remarkable Bond between the Family of Teen Who Died in Ski Tragedy and the Woman Who Received Her Heart," DailyMail.com, April 11, 2013, https://www.dailymail.co.uk/news/article-2307594/Taylor-Storch-The-remarkable-bond-family-teen-died-ski-tragedy-woman-received-heart.html.
3. Meghan Holohan, "Parents Who Donated Late Daughter's Organs: 'It Was the Right Choice,'" May 11, 2013, https://www.today.com/health

/parents-who-donated-late-daughters-organs-it-was-right-choice-1c
9881412.

4. Todd and Tara Storch, parents of Taylor and founders of Taylor's Gift Foundation (www.TaylorsGift.org), tell the ongoing story of their journey of regifting life, renewing health, and restoring families in their book with Jennifer Schuchmann, *Taylor's Gift: A Courageous Story of Giving Life and Renewing Hope,* from Revell Books, a division of Baker Publishing Group, 2013.

5. Meghan Holohan, "Parents Who Donated Late Daughter's Organs."

6. Tara Storch, Outlive Yourself, http://www.tarastorch.com/#home.

UNFATHOMABLE FORGIVENESS

1. Victoria Ruvolo, The Forgiveness Project, https://www.theforgivenessproject
.com/stories-library/victoria-ruvolo/, accessed September 10, 2023.

2. "Victoria Ruvolo, Who Forgave Her Attacker, Is Dead at 59," *New York Times*, March 28, 2019, https://www.nytimes.com/2019/03/28/obituaries
/victoria-ruvolo-dead.html.

A SIMPLE ACT OF KINDNESS

1. Michael Quintanilla, "Angel Gives Dying Father Wedding Moment," *San Antonio Express-News*, December 15, 2010. Used by permission of Chrysalis Autry.

2. Chrysalis Autry.

AMBITION SURRENDERED

1. Matt Lauer, "Miracle on Mount Everest," *Dateline* NBC, June 25, 2006, https://www.nbcnews.com/id/wbna13543799.

2. Matt Lauer, "Miracle on Mount Everest," *Dateline* NBC.

I GOT YOU

1. Gary Morley and Lisa Cohen, "Kayla Montgomery: Young Runner's Brave Battle with MS," CNN, May 20, 2015, https://www.cnn.com/2015/05/20
/sport/kayla-montgomery-multiple-sclerosis-athletics-feat/index.html.

2. Used with permission of Kayla Montgomery.

A HEART FOR THE CHILDREN

1. "Biography of Sir Nicholas Winton," Sir Nicholas Winton Memorial Trust, https://www.nicholaswinton.com/biography. Accessed September 10, 2023.

2. "Nicholas Winton, the Power of Good," Gelman Educational Foundation, May 28, 2009. www.powerofgood.net/story.php, and Patrick D. Odum, "Gratitude That Costs Us Something," heartlight.org/articles/200909/20090922_gratitude.html.

MORE THAN A GAME

1. Mimi Elliott, "Kris Hogan: Hogan's Heroes Fill Football Stands," CBN, 700 Club, September 17, 2013, https://www1.cbn.com/700club/kris-hogan-hogans-heroes-fill-football-stands.
2. Rick Reilly, "Life of Reilly: Gainesville State High School Football Gets the Best Gift of all: Hope," ESPN.com, December 23, 2008, http://sports.espn.go.com/espnmag/story?section=magazine&id=3789373.

NEW DREAMS

1. Lindsey Bradford, "Soldier's life altering injury turns into unique war love story," U.S. Army, January 8, 2010, https://www.army.mil/article/32624/soldiers_life_altering_injury_turns_into_unique_war_love_story.
2. Jay Kirk, "Burning Man," GQ.com, January 31, 2012, www.gq.com/news-politics/newsmakers/201202/burning-man-sam-brown-jay-kirk-gq-february-2012, 108–15; Sam Brown, personal conversation with the author. Used by permission.
3. "Sam Brown: A Story of Gratitude," Sam Brown for Nevada, 2023, https://captainsambrowngratitude.com/.

A MISSION OF MERCY

1. Thomas Lake, "The Way It Should Be: The Story of an Athlete's Singular Gesture Continues to Inspire. Careful, Though, It Will Make You Cry," *Sports Illustrated*, June 29, 2009, www.si.com/vault/2009/06/29/105832485/the-way-it-should-be.
2. Lake, "The Way It Should Be."

THE BURDEN OF DISCONTENT

1. Chris Seidman, *Little Buddy: What a Rookie Father Learned About God from the Birth of His Son* (Orange, Calif.: New Leaf Books, 2001), 138. Used with permission.

NOTES

I NEED HELP
1. Helen Roseveare, *Living Faith: Willing to Be Stirred as a Pot of Paint* (Fearn, UK: Christian Focus Publications, 2007), 56–58.

THE POWER OF PRAYER
1. "A Rodeo Cowboy's Fight to Survive," August 20, 2012, CBN.com. The Christian Broadcasting Network Inc. Used with permission. All rights reserved. http://www.cbn.com/tv/1794454498001. The full story is recounted in Freddy Vest, *The Day I Died: My Breathtaking Trip to Heaven and Back* (Lake Mary, Florida: Charisma House, 2014).

ROCK-STAR CAREGIVERS
1. "COVID-19 Patient Writes Inspiring Message on Glass to Caregivers," Cleveland Clinic, 2023, https://my.clevelandclinic.org/patient-stories/375-covid-19-patient-writes-inspiring-message-on-glass-to-caregivers. Accessed September 10, 2023.
2. "COVID-19 Patient Writes Inspiring Message on Glass to Caregivers," Cleveland Clinic, March 28, 2020, YouTube, https://www.youtube.com/watch?v=pIzNAgiBETM.

MR. HAPPY MAN
1. "Mr. Happy Man—Johnny Barnes," YouTube, https://www.youtube.com/watch?v=v_EX5NzqNXc. See also Jarrod Stackelroth, "Mr. Happy Man," Adventist Record, July 21, 2016, https://record.adventistchurch.com/2016/07/21/mr-happy-man/.
2. Raj Bjattacharya, "Johnny Barnes, Mr. Happy Man of Bermuda," Bermuda Attractions, Bermuda Ebooks and Travel Guides, https://www.bermuda-attractions.com/bermuda2_0000bf.htm. Accessed September 10, 2023.

SANDWICHES AND WISDOM
1. Andrew Shain, "As He Heads to the U.S. Senate, Tim Scott Praises Early Mentor," *Beaufort Gazette*, July 2, 2013, http://www.islandpacket.com/news/local/community/beaufort-news/article33492450.html.
2. Tim Scott, "Entrepreneur Took Time to Teach Life Lessons on Taking Responsibility," *Post and Courier,* January 3, 2010, updated December 8, 2016, https://www.postandcourier.com/news/special_reports/entrepreneur

-took-time-to-teach-life-lessons-on-taking-responsibility/article_9b2a2c5d
-ce82–5ac4-be65-f83753ed2231.html.

THE POWER POSTURE

1. Eben Alexander, *Proof of Heaven: A Neurosurgeon's Journey into the Afterlife* (New York: Simon and Schuster, 2012), 38, 45–46, 103.

BREAKING BREAD

1. Email correspondence to me from Brian Reed on February 21, 2016. Used by permission.

MAKE SOMEONE HAPPY

1. John Feinstein, "How Jake Olson of USC Became the Most Famous Long Snapper in College Football," *Washington Post*, September 5, 2017, https://www.washingtonpost.com/sports/colleges/how-jake-olson-of-usc-became-the-most-famous-long-snapper-in-college-football/2017/09/05/900672f0–923a-11e7–8754-d478688d23b4_story.html.
2. "Jake Olson: Longsnapper and Speaker," https://jakeolson.me/.

SELFLESS LOVE

1. Maxie D. Dunnam, *This Is Christianity* (Nashville: Abingdon Press, 1994), 60–61.

A BRAVE VOLUNTEER

1. Paul Aurandt, ed., *More of Paul Harvey's The Rest of the Story* (New York: Bantam Books, 1980), 79,-80.

HANDCUFFED BY LOVE

1. Charles Colson, "Making the World Safe for Religion," *Christianity Today*, November 8, 1993, 33.

UNFAILING LOVE

1. Nicole Wiesensee Egan, "Mom Who Saved Her Children from Tornado Has No Regrets About Losing Her Legs 'It Was My Time to Step Up,'" *People*, March 9, 2017, https://people.com/human-interest/stephanie-decker-mom-saved-children-tornado-lost-legs/.